NABILA GERON

DESPERATELY

SEEKING

SEX

N

G

Bookalicious Group Inc.

ISBN 978-1-09833-814-5

AUTHOR'S NOTE

Please Be Advised: The following book is intended for mature and insensitive audiences and contains Adult Content, Strong Sexual Content, and Offensive Language. Like, I'll leave it up to you... But... You gotta know about this stuff before getting into this whole thing you know?

To the reader:

WARNING

If you dare to read this story, you become a
percipient.

A person who has a good understanding of things;
perceptive. Thank you

DORITO JAY

(timeframe: 1984 – 1993)

Dear Isa,

I was born with Treacher Collins Syndrome in December of 1970. Microtia ears made me deaf, which was why I had to wear bone-conduction hearing aids. They didn't make them anymore. I was a light-skinned black female, with thick, shoulder-length hair. I also had an elongated, protruding jaw, which was why some black children called me a monkey. My eyelids drooped. I weighed a hundred-pound and was five feet tall, with an average-looking body. I grew up in Memphis, Tennessee.

***

Marriage was never on my mind because I was around my mom and sister, who were not married. I didn't know how to live with a man. My father wasn't around. My mom brought men into the house. I could remember their names: Otis, Claiborne, and then Joe. My mom and my dad were divorced. When I was growing up, it seemed like every night she and a man were sitting on the couch, watching TV.

My sister was the same. I remembered her ex-boyfriends' names: Vincent, Patrick, and Vernon. I would walk into the living room, which had a dark orange, leather sofa to find my older sister, Phyllis, kissing a young man. But I never had a boyfriend and still don't. I didn't know how to French kiss.

My mother was a light-skinned Black, and my sister and I were, too. My mom was around forty-five years old. She always had short, thin hair and wore makeup. My sister was around twenty-one. She used to wear makeup and kept her hair short; her hair was thicker than my mom's. But my hair was thicker than my sister's. She was pretty and thin, with perky breasts. My mom had a nice face with some moles and a pudgy body.

I was around fifteen years old. I was never envious of them, with their love life and normal faces. I just thought it was normal for me.

I had many men later in my life. I never settled down. It seemed like every few years I have been with a man. I had never been in a love relationship. I have just had friends with benefits that were short-term. I never looked for a new man, men approached me.

I didn't know why some people think it was strange that I didn't have a boyfriend. They didn't understand my situation. No boy ever asked me out on a date. I was too ugly, I accepted that, no hard feelings. I didn't notice that I was different. Some people thought my life is just like theirs. But it's not.

***

In 1986, the yellow special Type B, twenty-four seats, 1980s bus came from the north and down the street, then parked in front of the driveway, waiting for me. I lived in the orange-reddish house with black bars on the windows and front door on Don Street. It was a middle-class neighborhood, with a mostly Black population in the Westwood area. We had a nice, beautiful, green lawn. It was fall, of course.

Rushing out the house, I hopped onto the bus, sitting nearly in the back. Resting my knees up against the back of the seat, sitting in the fetus position, I decided to sit on the right side this time.

I felt like going to school was endless. But it was the first day of school. I was in seventh grade. The bus driver took a left on Parkrose, passing by Mount Vernon church, then right onto Ford Road. It seemed like the same route we took last year, going to Richland Elementary. After picking up Samuel and Danny, the bus driver took a different route from what we had ever taken. I wondered who the bus driver was picking up. We entered the Westhaven area, on Shelby Drive, turning left on Neely Road, and then another left I believe. I don't remember the street well. But I always drove to his house by memory. I can read and write. But I just don't remember the name of the street he lived on.

The boy, Jay, was sitting on the left side of the bus, always smiled after he looked back at me. He was in the third row. I was in the fifth row. He seemed cute, with curly, short black hair and light-skinned black. I just ignored him.

I never spoke to Jay. He looked back to glance and smile at me every ten minutes. I didn't know why.

I enjoyed the bus ride from Don Street to Mason, twenty-six miles. But the bus picked up twenty students, one by one. It took two hours to get to school. I didn't mind, because I had a cute boy, Jay who I could look at every weekday.

The bus dropped some of us, including me, off first at White Station Middle School. Jay and the other kids were dropped off somewhere else because he was much younger than me, around twelve years old. White Station Middle School was on 5465 Mason Road in Memphis and was about ninety percent of white students when I went there.

***

The room for the hearing impaired was in a trailer, separated from the normal children. The hearing-impaired children are separated from normal children. I felt segregated as if I was in the 1960s. The only time I got to blend in with the normal children was when I went to mainstream classes, which meant there would be three or four of us hearing impaired in a class full of normal classmates with a sign language interpreter, sitting up front, on the far side. The interpreter was never in the middle section or the back of the class.

I was so happy to finally leave Richland Elementary on 5440 Rich Road in Memphis. I knew I should have been in high school at the age of fifteen, but I was kept in Richland Elementary for what felt like forever. The teachers kept saying that I wasn't ready. They were being so ignorant. My facial appearance doesn't affect my brain. I told them that if they didn't let me leave Richland Elementary, I wouldn't study anymore. I was done. So, they finally let me go to White Station Middle School.

Our trailers there were parked between Richland Elementary and White Station Middle School at J J Brennan Park.

I was with a nice brunette, Mrs. Regan. She looked more like Rachael Ray from the Food Network. It was nice to be in a new environment, meeting new people.

***

When I got to White Station Middle School, I had an English class with Mrs. Mosby. I met hearing impaired classmates Michelle and Robbie, and the ASL interpreter, Nancy. And the rest of my twenty classmates were hearing.

English was tough for me. I couldn't really read. I was thinking that as long as I know where to put the "s", "ed", was, am, and stuff like that, but I didn't know the rest of the English-language structure. I couldn't understand the sentence at all. It seemed like I went from third-grade English level to seventh-grade English level.

The ASL interpreter, Nancy, had this long, brunette hair, about thirteen inches, covering up her breasts. She was white, nearly heavy set. She helped me.

She proofread my papers and gave them back to me. "Wrong, correct it again."

I stared at the sentence for five minutes, trying to find out what error I missed. I read the sentence but never knew what the sentence meant. I looked for whether I needed to put an "s" or "ed" or not. I was very thankful for Nancy who was also a special ed teacher.

***

I did make friends with the normal students, the twins, Nina and Tina, and Stephanie. Michelle and I always sat with them at the table in the cafeteria.

***

Then there was Joe. Joe married my mother in April of 1985. There was also my stepsister Shauna. They both were dark-skinned black, with a brownish color skin tone.

I was older than Shauna. Shauna was an average body type, but she was taller than me. Joe had a robust beer belly, and always having a goatee.

The orange couch was gone, replaced with a beige floral sofa bed. My sister Phyllis joined the Navy. I had a new sister, Shauna, to tolerate. My life was changing dramatically like I had started another life.

I never thought Joe was going to be my stepfather. I thought he was going to go away, like Otis and Claiborne.

Otis had afro hairstyle; Phyllis called him a football head. He was light-skinned, too, caramel-like me. And Claiborne, who was overweight, had a brown skin tone. What I liked most about him is his album collection. I only liked listening to Michael Jackson's *"Off the wall"* album. I didn't remember ever hearing those songs on the radio in the car.

I was so thankful for Joe. I really was. I didn't realize he was a true friend and wanted to be family to me. He really accepted me for who I was. Sadly, I gave him a hard time. Phyllis and Shauna acted like they didn't really appreciate me. I felt like Cinderella.

***

From 1987 to 1989, I had to go to White Station High School, which was on 514 South Perkins Road in Memphis. I didn't understand why they had White Station High School and White Station Middle School, they might as well have a White Station Elementary School.

I had ridden the yellow bus, which drove up to someone's house and picked up a hearing-impaired student. The bus was no longer going to Jay's house. Instead, we went straight to Oakshire Elementary School to pick up Michelle, who was from Hernando, Mississippi. Her mother drove from Hernando to Memphis and parked in Oakshire's parking lot. The bus driver picked up Michelle and then went on to the school. No JAY. Jay wasn't on the bus anymore. I was so sad.

Michelle and I became close friends. Her skin was so pale, and she had wavy, medium-length, blondish brown hair. I also didn't see Robbie. He had braces and was an average-looking white teenager. I figured he had probably gone to the Tennessee School for the Deaf.

***

Every time the yellow bus parked in front of Berenda's house, we had to wait over thirty minutes for her to get ready. Her older brother would have to wake her up and they would be in a fight. The bus driver kept honking the horn every five minutes. The bus driver was a slightly overweight, dark-skinned black woman with jerry curls.

She was short-tempered. "I'mma leave, seems like every day with this girl."

If I were the bus driver, I would have left her. The bus driver shouldn't have to wait for Berenda for more than five minutes. Every day, we waited around thirty minutes for Berenda to wake up, put on clothes, and hurry up to get on the bus.

Berenda finally climbed into the bus, crying, and sometimes sitting next to me.

"Scoot over, scoot over, god damnit, I hate school!!" she whined.

Her mom named her Berenda instead of Brenda. She was six feet tall, with wide hips. She needed the whole seat for herself. But the yellow bus was nearly packed.

***

I met some people I had seen at Richland Elementary and new hearing-impaired people, but no Jay. There was Emil, who was my favorite, with nearly light skin in a brownish copper skin tone. He always told funny stories and made people laugh. He seemed like a natural comedian, and it seemed like he could work on a comedy show. I didn't know how much he could hear, but he could talk and had a football player-type body.

I also saw a few other people, like Poorna, Neisha, Alex, and Gary who had gone to Richland Elementary. They were a little older than I was, so I thought I would never see them again. The Elementary school special ed. teachers really held me back. I was around seventeen and in ninth grade. I should have been in eleventh or twelfth grade with them.

I also met Chris, he was a light brown skin tone handsome guy. Alex used to live on Bonwood, the cross street of Don Street. He was handsome, but he had a cross-eyed. And then there was Deidre, a dark-skinned, pretty Black girl. But still no Jay. Gary was a dark-skinned Black male who always seemed so girlish. Neisha was a pretty White girl with blonde hair with blue eyes. She was pregnant in high school, like eight months pregnant. So, I figure she wouldn't be going to college. Poorna, who was from India, and I never could understand why her hair was so jet black, but it was long and looked like a white girl's hair. I put a whole jar of grease on my nappy hair to make it like that, but it didn't work.

Then I saw Darryl, a light-skinned, handsome, young, Black man.

***

White Station High School was also ninety percent white students, and it was eight minutes away from White Station Middle School. I spent most of my high school learning English and math, or at least it felt like it. I was so tired of school. By then I was nearly eighteen years old. I didn't know many eighteen-year-old students, most were graduated at that age. It seemed like I had been to school forever.

My grades were bad, and my home life was boring as well. I had a few mainstream classes with ASL interpreters and a few classes with the special ed teachers. It seemed like the special ed classes were easier than the mainstream classes. I laughed at the hearing impaired in the special ed classes, showing off how smart I was. But in the mainstream classes, I had to compete with the hearing kids. The hearing, the classmates who could hear normally and had no problem with their ears, were way ahead of me, especially in English classes. I didn't understand why I couldn't be in a special education English classes. My grammar was so terrible. I didn't know why they kept assigning me to mainstream English classes, especially with Mrs. Young who was my ASL interpreter, I felt she really didn't like me at all.

***

In the fall of 1988, when I was in the tenth grade, and guess who was in high school? Jay. I still ignored him. I didn't think I would ever see him again. I was nearly eighteen years old, and I was ready to leave school. It was so boring.

***

In November, I ran away from home and went to Los Angeles by Greyhound bus with my two parakeets, using my mom's credit card. I came back to Memphis by plane because my mom and Uncle Warren told me I have to go back. When I walked into the house, there were so many people there to console my mom, because Joe had passed away.

***

At White Station High School, my special ed counselor, Mrs. Gross, sat me down in her office. Mrs. Gross was in her forties, a white woman with average body shape, and wore her brunette hair in a short style.

"How do you think you're going to live in California with no money?"

"I don't know, I didn't think about it," I said.

At the age of seventeen, I was naive. I learned something. I think that running away from home to go to California wasn't a bad idea; it was good to have some experience about what California was like, instead of daydreaming about how life was in California. With what I learned about California—the appearance of Los Angeles scenery, trash, the number of homeless people, the housing expense—my hopes and dreams about moving there diminished. I saw reality. If I didn't go sooner, I would've done something stupid such as dropping out of school. I saw that I needed money. I needed a job. So, I decided to stay in school to work on that goal.

But then there was Jay. He playfully grabbed me in the hallway. That really took my mind off of California. Jay wasn't little anymore. Not as cute as he was. But in his charming way, it made him more attractive. He was taller than me with a high-top hairstyle which was a trend. Jay was really a laidback, down-to-earth guy. I really liked him. I guess I got his attention by running away. Attention from Jay was the only benefit I got from running away. I never had a crush before. But I wouldn't keep my hopes up. So, I continued to ignore him.

***

The next day, Jay blocked my path, flirting with me. Boys have never done that to me. Boys would look at me with disgust, especially the dark-skinned, black guys. I remembered Anthony saying a few months ago.

"Come back with a different face!"

It was on the last day of school because I was supposed to go to Boston the next day with my mother to have reconstruction surgery at Boston's Children's Hospital.

My protruding jaws were surgically pushed back and I was now looking much better. But still, my face looked different from the normal person's face. The surgery was a major one; the doctors spent hours reconstructing my face. I lost so much blood, causing me to have iron deficiency anemia, which will have long-term effects on my health. That's why I felt like I was entitled to have a better life after what I had gone through.

***

Because of Jay, I like light-skinned, black boys. He made me feel more confident to flirt back with him. Wow.

Every day I said to him. "Hey, Jay!"

He would reach out to me and give me a big hug. I was thinking, forget California. I love school again. I liked my life now. Jay really changed my life. Allowing me to express myself by flirting with him. But I still kept my guard up, because it seemed too good to be true. I tested him to see how much he could tolerate me. But he seemed so limitless. I would pull down his polyester All-black-red-and-yellow-stripes shirt, to peek at his nipple.

"Ooooo, girl," he said.

I grinned.

***

Finally, I got my driving license around 1989 or 1990 and my mom lent me a blue 1985 car, Chrysler LeBaron. I later colored it gray. I thought it would be like silver, but it was a dull gray as if someone used house paint to paint the car. My mother had offered to paint it.

"Gray," I said.

Happily, I would drive to school in it. I offered someone a ride and I ended up taking home four people. Of course, Jay, Savannah, Berenda, and Danny. I met Savannah and Danny at Lincoln Elementary in 1976.

A few days later, I told Berenda that I couldn't take her home because I had a hair salon appointment.

She yelled at me. "I don't care!"

"Hurry up and get on the yellow bus before it leaves," I told her.

She finally got out of my car. Because she lived far away from my house, I allowed only Danny, Jay, and Savannah as they lived so close to me.

Danny was five feet two inches tall, dark-skinned black, but he never caused me a problem. He looked more like Kevin Hart. Sometimes he would ride with me. Savannah was pretty-looking, but always slightly overweight.

"She's jealous of you," Jay said.

"Why?" I asked.

"Because you are with me," he said.

We weren't boyfriend and girlfriend. Jay and I were just friends. He was my crush. That's it. She could have him if she wanted to. She would almost look like the actress Gabrielle Union if she was thinner. One day she would get married and have children. But I know I won't have that. I just know it because of the way I look.

***

At home, I watched music videos on BET, VH1, and MTV. I sat on the wooden stool near the dresser in my blue-walled bedroom. The TV sat on top of the dresser.

When the video, *"Kissing game"* sang by Hi-Five came on, I cried. "I wish I could marry Jay."

My mother saw me across the hallway from her pinkish bedroom.

"Why are you crying?" she asked.

"Nothing," I answered.

***

During the summer, I asked Jay and Savannah if we could go to a drive-in theater; they both agreed. So, I went to Jay's brown-bricked house. He asked me to come in to speak to his sister. His sister didn't look like him at all; just an average-looking, black woman with a fat stomach. I sat on the sofa in the living room with Jay and his sister. The sister wanted to get to know me.

After we chatted a bit, she looked at me. "Where is Savannah?"

I was a bit sad but didn't let that bother me much. I didn't know why she mentioned Savannah. I felt like that was a rejection, so I couldn't marry into the family.

Jay and I were then on our way to Savannah's white parallel shotgun 1930s house. She lived with her ten siblings and her mother. I didn't know what poverty was. I thought nothing of it. I just thought Savannah was the coolest person ever because of her gold teeth, pretty-short permed gel hairstyle, and her ghetto ways.

We all went to the Malco Southwest Twin Drive-In movie theater; it was just five minutes away from my house, in the Westwood area, one of the coolest places in Memphis that I loved to go to. I missed going to the Drive-In with my sister and mom when I was younger. I believe it closed in 2001. If I were a millionaire, I would reopen that place.

So, I parked my car and put the speaker on the door's window, before the movie started, I asked Savannah and Jay if they wanted something at the concession store. Jay decided to come with me. I bought popcorn, drinks, and candies.

"Look Who's Talking" started to play. Jay decided to sit in the back with Savannah. And while the movie was on, they were making out in the backseat. Which is why I don't have friends. I don't see the point of having friends. People hate me now, for not being their friend. Why do I need friends who don't care about my feelings? People might say they aren't like that, but I know that they will subconsciously.

I enjoyed the movie, ate the popcorn, and drank a large cup of Coca-Cola with ice. Sprayed 'Off' bug spray on my skin, to ward off mosquitoes. Savannah, Jay, and I were hearing-impaired, but we had our hearing aids. We didn't have a closed caption to hear the actors clearly.

Closed caption television probably was in store, but we wouldn't know about it. It was the 1990s. I really don't think Savannah and Jay understood the movies I was taking them to. They weren't completely deaf, they could hear about fifty percent. That was why I always turned the volume way up to the maximum so all of us to hear the movie. They talked like a normal person, but I suffered from a little speech impairment.

***

In 1991, I decided to hang out with my other friends. Especially James, who dug his nose every three minutes. I sat next to James in the High School Auditorium. We were supposed to listen to each candidate who is running for high school class president. Handsome, caramel-colored skin complexioned Corey was at the podium in the middle of the stage, giving out the campaign speech, with the sign language interpreter on the far side of the stage. James was a dark-skinned black, average-looking guy, he looked like Ahmaud Arbery. He couldn't talk at all and he was totally deaf.

I peeked over to James.

"Cute," he signed about five times.

So now I figured he was gay.

In class, James wrote a note, then he gave Corey the note in the hallway. The other black guys who were with Corey looked at each other.

"He's gay, man," they said to Corey.

Sadly, James didn't hear that. I drove James home in my car. I didn't know he lived in a poor area. The train track ran in front of his house. Luckily, he was deaf, and the train noise didn't disturb his sleep.

One day, James invited me to go to a party at his house. Savannah wanted to come along, so I picked her up. As we got there, we could hear loud music playing, James and his braless sister were dancing. Her titties were just jingling around inside her white tank top.

I saw Evon, a light-skinned Black girl with sores on her body, mostly on her arms. She was kind of pretty. I believe she had eczema or psoriasis. Evon dropped out of school and had cute babies. She was deaf, as well. The last time I saw her was at my church, Harris Memorial on Ely Street. Then the church moved somewhere else because of the stair, the elderly couldn't get up the stairs to get to the front door.

People in the Deaf community in Memphis were mostly poor and Black. And they have kids. They don't go to college. Partying and having babies were all they did. That was why I didn't want to be like that. Savannah, Tracy, and Berenda decided to stay in Memphis and have babies, but I decided to go to Gallaudet in 1991 because I know that there is more in life than making babies. There had to be some opportunities out there for me.

***

Jay was talking to me again. I guess after seeing me with Savannah in the school hallway. I just wasn't the type of person to get mad over nonsense. I don't fight over a man.

"Can I kiss you?" I asked him before school started.

He parked my car near the gym, where nobody can see us.

He pointed at his cheek. "Right here."

So, I kissed him on the cheek.

"Thank you," I smiled.

After school, Jay hopped in my car and I asked him if we could try sex.

"Okay," He nodded.

I drove to my house, but I was nervous. We walked through the house, all the way to the back. Beside my yellow, twin-sized bed, we pulled down our pants.

"I'm ready," Jay said.

I gave him the condom and he unwrapped it. He wouldn't show me his penis. I don't know what it looked like. So, I laid down and spread my legs, and he got on top. He struggled to put his penis in.

I was just impatient. "Let me get on top."

"Don't look at it," he said.

I patted around. "Oh there."

Trying to insert his penis inside in my hole. I was struggling, too.

I had to screw it in there. "Ouch, that's hurt."

So, I just humped on it a bit. I didn't feel anything.

I heard Jay moaning a bit. "Okay, that's enough. I got to go to the bathroom."

We got up and put our pants back on and he went into the bathroom and closed the door. My mother wasn't at home. She was at work at Westhaven School, where she worked as a third-grade teacher.

I heard the doorbell and went up front to the living room to open the door. My cousin Daphne was at the door. I let her in, but I forgot why she was there. Maybe to spy on me, or to tell me something about the prom. She allowed her fiancé to take me to the prom. Jay came into the living room, and I introduced him to her.

"That's my friend, Jay."

She didn't need to know anything else.

I was twenty years old and he was seventeen. I read in the news about statutory rape recently, when I looked back at the time I had sex with Jay, I could have gone to jail. I guess it wasn't a big deal back then, or nobody knew about the law. But now it is. I wonder if Jay can sue me or some prosecutors might want to put me in jail for that.

Jay thought Danny and I had sex.

"Not really, we kept our pants on, we were just grinding on the school bus. Even with Darryl. But we were like seven years old and ten years old," I told him.

I think an adult molested Darryl, and because of that he sexually touched Savannah and me and motivated Danny to do the same. I never thought it was wrong. But sexual intercourse with Jay, oh my, I was so happy, to finally not be a virgin anymore. I think Jay was a virgin too because he didn't know what he was doing down there. I just felt like the regular people, having sex. I felt so normal.

Later, my stomach was acting up, so I drove to the store to buy a pregnancy test. I opened the pregnancy test package, saw the pregnancy test kit, and thought this was an odd-looking thing. I followed the instruction and it was negative. Yeah, I was sad and disappointed. I still thought I might be pregnant.

***

I told people at school, even James.

"What size was his penis?" James asked me.

"Um, I didn't look at it, Jay wouldn't let me. Maybe six inches," I answered.

I used my fingers to demonstrate how long it was.

I told Berenda, who sat behind me in English class. "I think I might be pregnant."

Berenda banged my body against the desk I was sitting on, over and over again. She faked laughing and then frowned at me as she banged my upper body with her hand. I didn't know if she truly cared about me or was jealous of me. She was being a hypocrite because she was pregnant. She reminded me of Esther on the TV show "*Sanford and Son*", Berenda looked so much like her, but she wasn't old.

Savannah walked up to me in the hallway. "Did you have sex with Jay?"

"Yes," I told her.

She didn't say anything else after that. She paused. She was through with Jay.

Jay walked up to me. "Why are you telling everybody?"

"Oh, I can't tell anyone?" I asked.

He was a little upset.

Later, I saw Savannah with Clay. Clay was also deaf, nice looking with a copper-like skin tone. He had a car and a job. Clay parked his car at the back of the High School and Savannah hopped in. I guess I didn't have to drop her off home anymore.

***

A few days later, I went to Libertyland, and
Savannah, Tracy, James, and my other deaf friends came
along. We went on the roller coaster and Tracy lost her
glasses. I didn't know if it was her first time because she
should have known the ride would've made her glasses fly
off. I put my hearing aid and glasses in my purse before
the roller coaster vehicle moved.

We went up to the water slide and Tracy slid
down without her glasses. I took Tracy home and she
invited me and Savannah inside. She gave us a house tour.

Tracy signed it to her mother. "I lost my glasses."

"What? How did you lose them?" her mom asked.

Tracy was reading lips because she was tone deaf
and couldn't hear anything. Her overweight mother didn't
know sign language.

Savannah and I visited Tracy at her house, again.
Tracy showed us her eight-months pregnant belly with
ugly stretch marks. The stretch marks were so reddish
and bruised looking. I didn't know pregnancy could be
that ugly. Tracy was explaining she was scratching
because her belly was so itchy. I don't know why she
would get pregnant, because she had sickle cell blood
anemia. Her eyes were yellow, and she got sick sometimes
in the special ed classroom.

I felt like I would be going to college alone because most of my friends weren't going. Anyway, Tracy didn't have a job. I didn't know where her boyfriend was, and I wondered what he looked like. I didn't know why any man would be with her, she wasn't at all attractive. Tracy was slim but short. She lived in her momma's 1930s-looking house, near James's house which was on Southern Avenue, and I guess she will raise the baby there, living off of food stamps and stuff.

***

Miss. Beasly and I sat together in the classroom, on the desks.

"I think you should do twelfth grade, again. We don't think you should graduate," she said.

"I don't care, there's Jay, I don't mind going to school. I'll just flirt with Jay and having more sex with him. Maybe get pregnant by him," I lied.

I grinned. She looked at me for ten minutes. She was a tough, light-skinned heavy-set bitch, but I knew how to talk to her. I was twenty years old. If I spent another year in high school, that would mean I will be twenty-one years old when I graduate. That's why I felt like I spent so much time in school. My life was wasted. I could've been a junior in college by now. I don't know why these special education teachers kept deaf students in school for an extended period of time. Most of us deaf students aren't going to get the best job positions anyway. Most of us will live off of Social Security Income (SSI) or work in the post office and warehouses. Why keep us in school for so long?

***

I had to pass a history class in order to graduate. I buckled down and studied at home for hours on Joe's wooden dining room table, sitting on the wheeled white cloth seat, the one with the weak cushion due to Joe, who was overweight, sitting there for so long. Educating myself, asking my mom about what she knew about U.S. History.

My black ASL interpreter, the only black ASL interpreter at the school, couldn't do sign language at all. ASL stands for American Sign Language. But we had to keep a secret because she needed the check to provide for her family. Instead, she took notes, as a notetaker, while we hearing-impaired students looked around the classroom and sometimes daydreamed.

The next day, she gave us copies of the notes. I used those notes, I had never thrown them away, to study.

When the final exam came, I felt like I was prepared, the exam looked so easy. I was one of the first students to finish. Others probably thought I was a fool because I always got Fs on homework and tests.

The next day, the teacher, a white man who was also a football coach, called our names and everyone got their tests back and saw their scores. I hadn't gotten mine yet.

"Someone here made an A-plus," the teacher told everyone.

He held up the test. "Nabila, come up."

I got up and he gave me my test paper.

"Good job!" the teacher said.

Passing that final exam really helped me graduate in 1991.

***

I never did ask Jay to take me to the prom. But I told everyone that my cousin's fiancé was taking me out.

Michelle was surprised when I told them. She felt better when she thought that I didn't have a prom date.

She broke down and cried. "I want to go to the prom. I have nobody to take me."

Miss. Beasly gave her the box of tissues and had to cancel the algebra special ed class. All ten of us had to take a break.

At the prom, I had on a short, black prom dress with a deep V-neck. I wore black stockings and black size-seven shoes that hurt my size-nine feet. Thurman, my cousin's fiancé, was tall, slim, and handsome with brown skin. He was a model, but he quit and chose to be a fireman instead.

The prom was nicely decorated and had a D.J. And a great disco light. I sat with Thurman, my favorite interpreter Mrs. Haug; Chuck, and his girlfriend, Stephanie sat with us. I hadn't seen Stephanie since middle school. I was surprised to see Stephanie again. She was pregnant when she died in a car accident in 1997. She didn't marry Chuck. She married someone else. She was the daughter of the Channel 5 news weatherman Dave Brown.

Michelle's partner was a white, hearing-impaired midget. They were at the table with me as well at the prom. I think it was weird because I thought James was going to be her prom date. James and Michelle used to date, but it didn't work out.

I still have the photos with Thurman and I. They had a cute blue and pink backdrop with blue and pink balloons. Mrs. Lynch, who had been my teacher in both elementary and middle school showed up to take a picture with me. She used to have twenty-inch long, blonde hair, then she chopped it off to a short, curly hairstyle. She was the prettiest special ed teacher I ever had.

***

In 1993, Savannah and I attended Jay's graduation. I don't know why she wanted to be there. She was with Clay, her boyfriend. She didn't have a car, so I drove her there. We went up to Jay on stage, who was in his green gown and cap. I don't remember what we talked about.

I smiled. "Congratulations, Jay."

Savannah decided to go and I went with her. That was the last time I saw him, on stage outside of the high school's baseball field in his green graduation gown. I didn't know what was on Jay's mind. I didn't know what was on Savannah's mind. But I was thinking about Byron, and I was looking forward to another day at LeMoyne Owen College.

Nabby

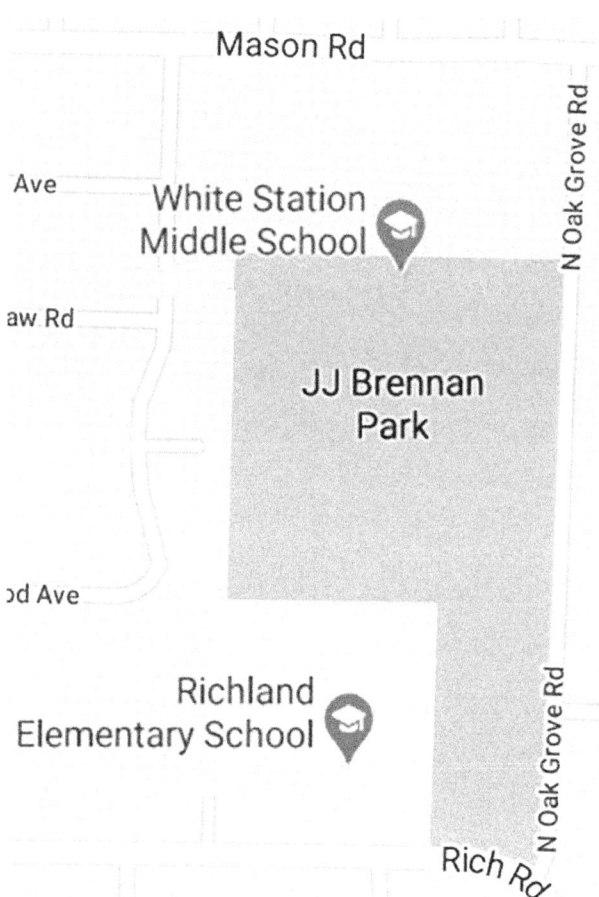

TYPE B JAY

Bone Conduction
Hearing Aids

RUN BY

(time frame: 1991 - 1994)

Dear Isa,

After I graduated from White Station High
School, I went to Gallaudet's School of Preparatory
Studies in Washington D.C., in the fall of 1991. Reason
why I chose this school, I wanted to know what it was
like to live in another city. It was located on 1640 Kalmia
Road, in Washington D.C. I was traveling from an
apartment in Gaithersburg, Maryland, where my sister
and I lived. She was stationed at the Navy base in
Bethesda, Maryland. Gaithersburg was thirty-six miles
away from Washington D.C., but Phyllis only had to drive
nineteen miles from Gaithersburg to Bethesda. I was so
tired of driving and getting stuck in traffic on the
interstate every morning, especially during the winter. I
had to leave thirty minutes earlier because the interstate
kept making me late getting to class. I read online that the
Preparatory School was closed in 1994.

***

I saw Gary there, but I hardly knew him. It was
good to see someone from high school. We were in
physical education class together, doing exercise, aerobic,
and survival skills at prep school. But I didn't really talk to
Gary that much.

***

Later, my sister wanted to take a Navy assignment in Spain and she wanted me to stay in a dorm. But I didn't want to, thinking that I would be treated badly by my roommates.

"No, you're not staying in this apartment alone!" Phyllis argued.

"Well I'm not staying in the dorm, I'll go back home with mom, then!" I said.

I really enjoyed studying at Gallaudet, and I made good grades. I really like Washington D.C., too. I wish I could have stayed there forever. But there was no way I would live in a dorm.

***

Gallaudet University was thirty miles away from Preparatory School. I tried to become a freshman at Gallaudet Univ. because I felt that the Prep School was a waste of time. During college enrollment, I filled out the registration application at the Registrar's Office and then sat down with the young white woman counselor. As she read my application and looked at my Prep School grades, she got up and tapped on the supervisor's shoulder.

"You have one more semester you have to finish at Preparatory," Supervisor said.

"Damn," I said to myself.

***

Near the end of spring semester, I was at the dorm building, a dark-skinned Black young deaf woman showed me around... touring me. The dorm rooms had bunk beds. Then she showed me a TTY machine. I had never seen one before. She turned it on and taught me how to use it. Then she showed me the shower room, and I saw the bottom of the shower, with three inches of mildew on the floor. It reminded me of the deaf camp I went to in Tennessee. I had to wear socks in the shower. I didn't want to step on that with my bare feet. I can see why people have athlete's foot. So, I would have to buy some flip flops. So, no, the tour of campus didn't change my mind. After the Preparatory School's spring semester was over, I argued with Phyllis again.

I sorta wish I hadn't left there. I could have stayed, maybe found out how to live in an off-campus apartment. But I didn't know anything about that. I didn't know much about SSI (Social Security Income). I should have known these things. I wish someone had told me. Maybe my life would've been much different. If I could turn back time, I would've fought for Social Security Income and gotten myself an apartment when I was twenty-one years old. But oh well. So, I left Washington D.C. and enrolled at LeMoyne Owen College in the fall semester of 1992.

***

During freshman orientation, in a very small auditorium located in the Alma C. Hanson Student Center, my mom and I had to listen to some guest speakers. After that was over, as I stood up, a curly-haired, biracial man with hazel eyes shook my hand.

"My name is Byron."

Because of that, I felt that I wouldn't regret not staying in Washington D.C.

***

LeMoyne Owen College is a Historical Black College and University (HBCU) in Memphis. My mother graduated from there before becoming a teacher. I decided to follow in her footsteps, but I was majoring in business administration.

I didn't have any ASL interpreter, so it was hard for me to hear. I wasn't doing so well at school. After my one o'clock class, Byron hugged me almost every weekday outside of the building. I don't know why, maybe because he felt sorry for me or that's just the kind of person he was.

Then one day there was Mimosa, a very beautiful woman with curly long hair standing near him. And oh-oh another Jay and Savannah situation. I decided not to hang out with Byron anymore. Just wave hi, hug, and go.

I didn't want to be rude, but I just didn't want to be in the triangle that would waste my time.

***

I liked the English class the best. We had a white professor with big eyes. The English class was easy. All I had to do was read some books and write an essay. I hated the computer class. I hadn't learned how to use a computer in the past. I didn't understand why computers were so important. It is a difficult machine. What is wrong with the typewriter? I decided to buy one for my own personal use. It was an IBM with a big monitor and desktop tower. I bought colorful floppy disks and a mouse, installed AOL, and engaged in conversation in chatrooms. The computer class was required.

***

Every day, I talked to Mom about Byron, and my sister heard me talking about it. She was on leave from her assignment in Spain. She still thought I should stay at the Gallaudet dorm.

"Can I go and meet Byron in person?" she asked.

"Yeah, okay."

I took Phyllis at LeMoyne Owen and gave her a tour around the campus. Then I saw Byron at Brownlee Hall talking with some people in the hallway, next to the

Administrative Office. I introduced him to Phyllis. They shook hands. As we turned around and was about to leave out the door.

"He's fat!" Phyllis said out loud.

I was hoping he didn't hear her.

"Phyllis was saying, 'He's fat!' and I don't know if he could hear her," I told my mother as soon as we got home.

My mom looked at Phyllis as she frowned. She knew better.

***

I went on to the accounting class, which was located at the Gibson-Orgill Mathematics and Science Learning Center (GOMASL). The professor didn't seem like he was interested in teaching. He just gave us assignments. Most of the time, he was absent. He was chubby with copper skin tone. I really didn't learn anything there. Then, all of a sudden, he never came back. We ended up with a replacement professor, which made it harder. It was near the end of the semester. LOC should've refunded my money, but I didn't think about it.

***

After I left the class, near the stairway, I noticed Mimosa's stomach. It has been a while since I had seen her. We chatted. I really want to know whose baby she was carrying. Maybe Byron's. It couldn't be, because the other day, Byron was talking about my body.

"Those hips!" he said.

I told him that I don't have hips, just a big butt. I don't know why Byron was wasting his time talking to me. He and Mimosa should go ahead and be together. They were beautiful. They would make a beautiful couple. I thought whoever Mimosa is having sex with wasn't the right person for her. I thought Byron should date someone like Mimosa. They both have curly hair and nice, pretty skin tone. Mimosa sort of looked like the singer Vanity, with that curly long hairstyle.

***

I visited Tony, my Vocational Rehab counselor at the One Commerce Square Building which was located on 40 South Main Street in Memphis. He was a white, average-looking tall brunette guy.

"Can I get a sign language interpreter?"

"Can you sign language?" he asked.

"Yes, I can," I answered.

"I don't think you need one. I can help you get a job," Tony said.

I left there empty-handed. Vocational Rehabilitation was used to only help people who became disabled in the military, through the VA (Veterans

Affairs). They helped people like me with disabilities as well, to fund a college education and job placement.

My grades were poor and VR would kick me out anyway. I thought about getting a job or joining the Job Corps.

***

The next day, I went to my professor's office. He was African. I could tell because of his last name and looks.

"My assistant can teach you computer."

I begged him to teach me.

I went upstairs with the assistant who was slightly overweight with brown skin complexion. She started tutoring me one-on-one. Her nose was running, There was no tissue. I think I hurt her feelings. I didn't mean to. I just wanted the professor to understand my disability and why I couldn't understand him. As I sat there next to her, her wet finger smeared the computer screen. I got a C in that class, and I still didn't know a lot about computers.

***

As I was driving on Interstate 69, heading to Interstate 55, in my blue 1987 Nova, I saw Mimosa driving her car with Byron ducked down in the passenger's seat. I still refused to hang out with Byron and Mimosa. I didn't want to be in a triangle. I didn't understand why he ducked down. He isn't my boyfriend. He could do whatever he wanted to and with any woman. I didn't wave at them. I just passed by them. I never offer Byron a ride in my car. I didn't want another Jay.

***

In front of the Brownlee Hall, there was a huge crowd. I didn't know what the event was about. Two tall women stood in front of me, but I wasn't moving. I just stood at the chosen spot. There was a white, blonde-haired woman at the podium, giving a speech. I won't vote for Democrat.

"I'm voting for Ross Perot," I told momma at home.

"You need to vote Democrat," she said.

"For what? We need businesses since I am majoring in Business Administration."

After the speech was over, the woman shook some people's hands and I tried to reach out. She missed my hands.

At home, I looked up online to see who that was. "Hillary Clinton?"

***

The next day, I was with Byron on campus.

"Can I see your dorm room?"

"Yeah, okay," Byron answered.

So, we walked, crossing the Walker Avenue, toward the dorm area, and finally, we were at the door. the 1960s—a projects-looking, brown brick, one-story building.

I was curious. I wanted to stay in the dorm, so I wouldn't have to drive from home to LOC. LeMoyne Owen College wasn't that far, just eighteen miles away.

"I lost my keys."

He knocked on the door, to see if his roommate was there.

I wondered if he had experience with sex. Maybe I should have asked him, flirted with him, since Jay was a virgin and he didn't do it right. I didn't think I will ever get married anyway. Why should I save myself? I didn't believe any man will want me for a wife. I wondered if I should have asked Byron for sex. Maybe I could learn what it feels like. I watched so many movies, and women acted like sex felt so good. But Nah, I didn't want to.

We walked back to campus, in front of Steele Hall.

"Can you help tutor me with my Accounting?" I asked.

"Sure," he answered.

"At the library, around lunch break?"

"Yes, I'll be there."

I remembered him offering to help me with my school lesson, so I thought maybe I would take advantage of the opportunity. Well, it was a nice walk with him.

***

At home on Don Street, I was watching the TV show, "*A Different World*", No closed caption, but I just watched it. The character Whitley was really funny. Darryl M. Bell who played Ron Johnson really reminded me of Byron. I was watching Ron kissing Freddie. Ron cheated on Kim. Kim's character was played by Charnele Brown, and Freddie was played by Cree Summer. I compared myself to Kim, even though she was very dark-skinned black. Freddie reminded me of Savannah and Mimosa, who knew that Kim likes Ron. He really liked Freddie, but Freddie was playing hard to get. Kim is like me—unaware and could someday be heartbroken.

***

I tested Byron, I was at the Hollis F. Price Memorial Library, waiting for him to show up to help tutor me. I looked at the clock as it passed at one o'clock. I was thinking, oh he was just being nice, hugging me as a friend. Now he's going to be a no show. I left the library and headed over to Vocational Rehabilitation.

***

At the VR, Tony introduced me to his assistant who was in the other cubicle office. He was tall, dark-skinned black, and handsome. I sat down with his assistant.

"Job Corps in Atlanta is the closest one near you, but they might not take you, because you're near twenty-four years old," he said.

"Well, my birthday is in December, so I won't be twenty-four most of the time in 1994 anyway."

Job Corps was located at 61 Forsyth Street in Atlanta, Georgia. They have one in Memphis, but it was full, so I had to go to Atlanta. I had never been to Atlanta, but I was excited to go. I wasn't doing well at all at LOC.

***

At LOC, I saw Byron. He gave me a hug and so I hugged him.

"Hey," I said and then I walked away.

I didn't stop to talk to him, since all he wanted to do is hug everybody. Okay, there was a hug. Okay, whatever. As I headed to my English class, which is on the second floor of Brownlee Hall, I just rolled my eyes.

Next day, I saw Byron, again. "I'll help tutor you, meet me at noon at the library."

"Okay!" I said.

I doubted it. I went on to accounting class. Only a few people were there, about six classmates. I couldn't hear the new professor. I heard that the old professor got arrested for stealing some money from the accounting room at the Administrative Office, but I didn't know if it was true.

***

The next day, I went to the library to see if Byron was really there. His face was scratched up as if a cat had scratched his face, or maybe a girlfriend that I didn't know about, scratched his face up. I don't know. Maybe he raped someone. He finally tutored me, but I wasn't learning anything. His facial injury really disturbed me.

***

At the academic advisor's office at LOC, I sat down with the advisor.

"I'm withdrawing. Is there some form that I need to fill out?"

She asked me instead of answering. "Why are you leaving?"

"I'm planning on going to Atlanta," I said.

"Atlanta?!"

She had helped me enroll at LOC and now she helped me exit LOC.

***

I said goodbye to Byron, and he gave me one last hug.

"I'm not coming back next semester; my grades are really poor," I said.

He was showing concern. It wasn't the last time I saw him either. I didn't say goodbye to Mimosa, because she wasn't around... probably at home with her new baby.

***

Driving away from LOC, I passed by the burned buildings from the Riot in 1968. Sadly, those buildings hadn't been demolished, and it had been nearly thirty years. What was up with that? We had a Black mayor, Mayor Herenton. He should have tried to make Memphis look better, especially around the LeMoyne Owen College area. Martin Luther King was shot in Memphis at the Lorraine Motel in 1968, located at 450 Mulberry Street. It was seven miles away from LOC. The mayor, though, would rather spend money on the downtown area.

Nabby

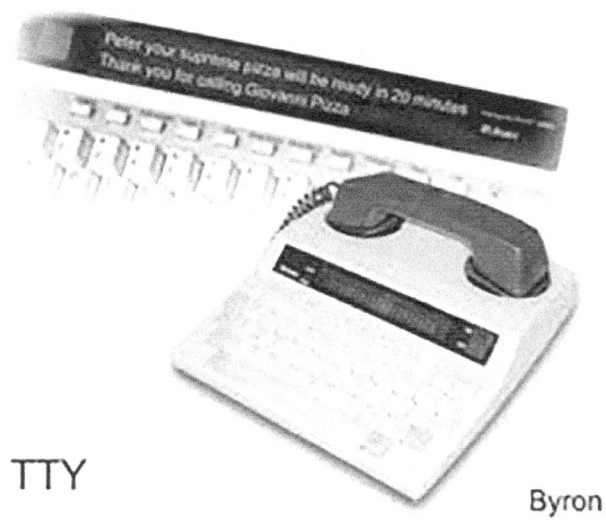

TTY

Byron

Prep
School

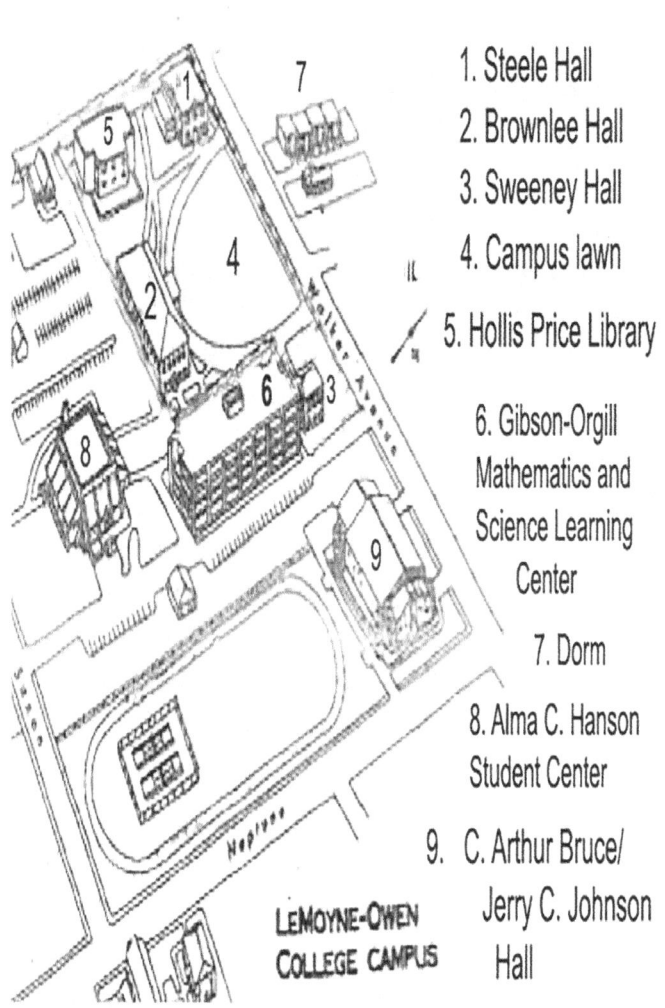

1. Steele Hall
2. Brownlee Hall
3. Sweeney Hall
4. Campus lawn
5. Hollis Price Library

6. Gibson-Orgill
   Mathematics and
   Science Learning
   Center

7. Dorm

8. Alma C. Hanson
   Student Center

9. C. Arthur Bruce/
   Jerry C. Johnson
   Hall

JEFF DUMBER

(timeframe: 1996 – 1997)

Dear Isa,

Fast-forward through the time I spent in Atlanta, fast-forward through the time I was at K-mart, fast-forward through the time I went to jail.

From 1991 to 1996, which was five years, I didn't have sex. A dog had more sex than I did. No men asked me out on a date. No men asked me for my hand in marriage. No men approached me. That's spelled N-O-N-E. I had no clue how to have a boyfriend. I didn't know what to do with a man. So, don't judge me. Don't pull out your Bible and start preaching. What would you have done if you were me, at age twenty-five, and had sex only one lousy time? Was I supposed to wait all of my life for a man?

***

I wanted to go to Gallaudet because I was curious about it. Gallaudet's Preparatory School wasn't the same as Gallaudet University. In the fall of 1996, during new student orientation at Gallaudet University, a school for the deaf and hard of hearing, I sat at the table, meeting with four deans who introduced me to various majors. I asked questions, as I was struggling to decide which subject I should major in.

One of them was Dr. Jane Norman, a blonde-haired, fifty-five-year-old woman. She was the dean of the Television, Film, and Photography (T.F.P.) department. I decided to major in TFP.

***

Walking into the TFP department felt like I was Dorothy walking out of the house and into Oz. Cameras, editing machines, and studio, oh my.

I was passing classes and enjoying my new life—except for my roommate. I had benefits from vocational rehab to pay for my education again. I loved the food at the cafeteria: the pizzas, wonton, sandwiches, and the drinks. It was so awesome. I saw Chris, Deidre, Poorna, and Alex, the cross-eyed man who lived on Bonwood again. And my cousin, Tasha, she was somewhat hearing impaired but could hear with her hearing aid. We interacted every now and then. But she was there just for one semester and then graduated from Gallaudet with a master's degree.

Chris used to go to Richland Elementary and White Station High School with me. I rarely saw him at Richland and WSHS. He was so quiet. Chris was a Gallaudet football player. A jock. His looks have nothing to do with anything. I could have asked anyone. I knew Chris, so I went to his dorm room and asked him to come to my dorm room to help me with something, and I wanted to give him the note. I was so nervous. I forgot what I had him to do. We stood near the bed. I think I saw him look at the note, which was laying on the bed, which read, "Can you help me with the sex?" Then he left. I decided to not ask anybody again for the rest of the fall semester.

***

In the Spring of 1997, in the Biology lab class, I was sitting next to Marcus on a stool. He was a football player too. He was dark-skinned, black, and handsome.

"May I borrow your book? I'll give it back to you at your dorm room," he asked.

"Okay," I gave him my book.

At my dorm room, I thought, "Well, maybe I can ask him for sex." Marcus knocked and flipped the light switch outside my door. The light switch is a doorbell for deaf people. It makes the light turn on and off inside the dorm room. I got up from my chair to answer the door and saw him standing in the hallway. He quickly handed me the book.

"Thank you," he signed.

He left. I didn't get a chance to ask him. I failed.

***

In Biology class, I stood next to the professor, who smiled at me and gave me my test paper.

"You're so smart!" she said.

She had given me an A on my test.

A few days later, someone tapped on my shoulder, while I was sitting on the fourth-row tiered seating in the Biology classroom.

"Hi, I'm Jeff. Can you tutor me in biology?"

"Okay, I live in Benson Hall. I'll write down my room number," I signed.

That was the time I regret. I really regret allowing this man into my life.

***

All I wanted was to know what sex was like. I didn't know he would change my life permanently. If I had stuck with humping pillows, my life wouldn't have changed at all. My goal was to see how sex really felt. His goal was to find a wife. It could also have been to break my heart or to hurt or lower my self-esteem so that the guys who were so unattractive could date me. I don't know. It seemed like in the deaf culture, if a man likes you, you had to do your hair, know how to cook, and be dressed up. My mother didn't teach me that. She didn't prepare me to find a husband. I went to Gallaudet to learn and to get an education.

I guess deaf men think if a woman makes an A in Biology, she can be a good housewife. If a woman can do a film, she can be a good housewife. If a woman is good at math, she can be a very good housewife. If a woman is very funny—no, she can't be on a comedy stage, she belongs at home as a housewife. I think that is what deaf men think.

I did tell Michael, a white classmate who was in my communication class, that I wanted a tall, curly-haired man, but I was just joking around. I guess he told other people what I said. Then, Jeff appeared.

***

I was in my dorm room, lying on my bed, thinking about how to ask him for sex without blowing it. I heard a knock. I had my biology book out. I answered the door and there was Jeff. I told him to come in. Jeff is a light-skinned black guy, maybe mixed with Hispanic since he said he was from California. It would've been nice to marry him and to move out to California with him since that state is my favorite place. His hair was curly with a ponytail. I didn't think he would marry someone like me. I didn't comb my hair for months, I kept it tucked under a hat. Yeah, I'm lazy. I was so independent.

I was staying in the dorm with no roommate. Adjusting the air conditioning and controlling the room temperature, I felt very comfortable.

Was I ready to ask him the question? Not yet. I placed the book on my lap, but he interrupted me. He was talking to me about things that weren't relevant to biology. I couldn't remember what he said.

"Are you living in a dorm?" I asked.

"Off-campus."

He could talk too. He signed and talked at the same time. I asked him if he could take me there. I was curious about the off campus apartment, because my sister and my mom should've allowed me to stay in one of those off-campus apartment instead of trying to get me to live in the dorm while I was at prep school.

"Yes, we can go now if you want to," he said.

"Well, I have a car. I can drop you off," I offered.

I grabbed my keys. Jeff picked up his one hundred pounds backpack and put it behind his back. We left out the building together. We didn't study at all together.

***

The dorm I was staying at was Benson Hall. Gallaudet was two miles away from the White House. I never went by the White House. I have been in

Washington, D.C., from 1991 to 1992, from 1996 to 1998, from 2000 to 2001 and then in 2003. All I saw were the Capitol Building, the Lincoln Memorial, Union Station, and the Jefferson Memorial. That's it.

Jeff's apartment was near Union Station. It seemed like the area was changing and being renovated. Construction workers were always out there, changing things every year for tourists.

At Jeff's apartment, we walked up the steps and turned right to the elevator. We went up and turned right. We walked all the way to the end of the hallway to his door. I don't remember the apartment number. I forced myself to forget that because I know I would go back there. I don't want to remember Jeff anymore, but it is hard to do.

We entered the apartment, and he held his eleven-toed cat away from the door so it wouldn't escape. He put down his one hundred pounds backpack by his desk. I looked around the room.

I flirted with him. "Can I kiss you on the cheek?" I stood on my toes in front of him and I gave him a kiss. He banged his crotch against mine as he laughed. "Wow, I guess I can go right ahead and ask him," I thought. As we sat on his bed, I saw a picture of a pretty, young white woman with short brown hair on his nightstand.

"Who is that girl in the picture?" I asked.

"My girlfriend," he signed.

I paused. At the time I was thinking that I would just ask him for sex and then leave.

"Can you have sex with me?" I blurted it out.

"No," he answered.

"Why?"

I guess I could ask someone else then. I was ready to leave there.

"I don't know you yet. I want to get to know you first," he answered.

I don't think he would like my criminal record. "Just ask again," I thought. I put my hand inside his pants and felt something hard. I pulled back quickly. I was wondering what that was. He laughed.

He rubbed my left breast. "Take off your shirt."

I took off my shirt.

"Take that off too," he said.

My breasts were saggy. I was feeling insecure, but I took off my bra. He laughed at them and rubbed them. I had to be naked in order to have sex with him. He took off his clothes. Wow, he had a nice body. I went in my purse and took out a condom, then gave it to him. He put it on, and it fit perfectly.

I laid down and he got on top. He was struggling to put his penis in. I thought this was another Jay moment. I thought I had to get on top of him, but he wouldn't let me.

He kept trying. "I can't."

I relaxed my sex organ's muscle. He pushed himself in. The pain was too much. I didn't know if it was the condom, or if his penis was too big. He was humping. I thought, "Wow, this is real sex." But I didn't know if he was doing it right, because he had mild cerebral palsy.

He took his penis out and took off the condom. I was ready to get up and go home, but he wanted me in another position. He wanted my head on the pillow and my legs toward up the ceiling. I told him I had another condom in my purse.

"No!" he yelled and forced his penis inside of me.

"Ouch!" I said.

I was not used to this. This was only my second time. I was not used to this at all. The pain was too hard to explain. My head was banging against the headboard about a hundred times as he fucked me so hard. It felt like it was an eternity. Did he rape me? I guess I deserved it.

I was hoping that I didn't become pregnant. I wasn't sure about my genes that could be passed on—and his genes too. It was kind of scary to think about it. Then, after he got through, he spilled his sperm all over my stomach and breasts. I touched the tip of his hard penis. It felt like a toy penis. That was such a fun experience.

"You can sleep here if you want," he signed.

He covered me with his white bedsheets.

"Okay," I said.

In the morning, the sun came up, and I woke up. Jeff was staring at me. I got up and put on my clothes.

"Thank you, that was fun," I said.

He got up as well and put on his clothes. I said goodbye to him, left his apartment, and drove back to the dorm room.

***

In my dorm room, I pulled down my pants and touched my vagina with my hand. The hole felt three inches wide. It was painful to walk. I didn't want to go to the biology class and see him again. I guess the actresses were phony about how good sex is. It didn't feel good at all. I was so disappointed. I didn't know why people made sex such a big deal. Or maybe I needed to get used to it.

***

In my scriptwriting class with about twelve people, there was a white female professor and a white female interpreter. I really loved the class, coming up with creative ideas and writing scripts while the professor waited for us to finish.

A tall, dark-haired white guy with a beard who sat next to me was looking at my script.

"That's boring," he signed.

I was writing a drama story. So, I guess I had to write something more creative and different. The next day, I sat on the other side of the classroom, and he again sat at the desk next to me. I wrote a new script almost like "*The Benny Hill Show*". He looked at my script.

"I don't know how the TFP department can do that," I signed.

"You will have to learn about editing," he responded.

"Do you watch Benny Hill?" I asked.

"No, but I know what you are talking about."

A few days later, the professor called the bearded guy to the front of the classroom with a video home system (VHS) tape in his left hand. He inserted the tape into the videocassette recorder (VCR) machine, showing the classroom his film project. Three white male students were acting, and the show was like Benny Hill. He hadn't given me credit and hadn't asked me to be involved in his project. I didn't tell the professor that he stole my ideas.

***

The TFP classes and the studios were all below Gallaudet's library. So, I went upstairs and looked up books on Treacher Collins syndrome (TCS). I saw there was a fifty percent chance that I could pass TCS genes to my child. And I looked at information on the Cerebral Palsy—same thing.

At the biology lab, the professor, who was white and had short hair with black-rimmed glasses, was giving us a microscope and a dish of DNA cells. If the DNA cell was deformed, we had to make a note of it and identify which cell has normal or abnormal chromosomes. He mentioned that the health clinic on the Gallaudet campus provided free genetic testing.

I walked from the Hall Memorial building to the health clinic, which was located next to the cafeteria, near Carlin Hall dormitory. They took my blood and told me to come back in a few weeks.

"We will notify you when the test result is back," the nurse signed.

***

I drove my car to the drugstore on 700 blocks of Florida, near Howard University, and purchased a bottle of folic acid tablets, in case Jeff and I had sex again without a condom. I had learned that folic acid could prevent birth defects.

I saw Jeff in the Benson Hall lobby. I sat down on the chair after a long day from the store. He stood eight feet away from me.

"Are you trying to get pregnant?" he asked me.

"No, but I might be."

"If you are, I will leave you."

I didn't know why Jeff thought that I was planning to get pregnant. I was the one who gave him a condom. He was the one that didn't want to put it on. He was the one who put that huge log forcefully inside my vagina. So, I didn't know why he thinks that way about me. He was the one who came to me. All I wanted was the sex, and that was it.

***

A few weeks went by. I returned to the health clinic and sat in the lobby to wait for my genetic result.

The nurse waved at me. "You can enter the office."

I sat down with the white doctor who looked like he was about fifty years old, had a beer belly and gray hair and beard.

"We couldn't find the TCOF1, POLR1C, or POLR1D genes that cause Treacher Collins syndrome. We don't know if you have TCS or not. Your DNA genes were probably mutated," he said.

"Did you bring the pictures of your parents and grandparents?" he then asked.

"Well, I don't have the picture of my dad's father, but my dad's mother looked normal, but I don't know how my dad's father looks like," I answered.

I showed him pictures of my parents, my mother's parents and my father's mother.

He looked at the picture carefully. "So, I guess, your genes were mutated."

"My mother thinks that my dad and she are cousins, and it may be the reason that I was born with this," I said.

He paused.

"Will my future children have this, whatever I have?" I then asked him.

"Yeah, fifty percent chance," he responded.

My plan to have children was off my list, because I didn't want my future children to go though hard life because of their appearance. I didn't know about in-vitro fertilization (IVF), egg retrieval, and Ultrasound then. But most men and I probably wouldn't be able to afford it, anyway.

***

I was headed to the TFP department at the Merrill Learning Center, which had the library and the

TFP studio and classes. Jeff blocked my path. Blocking between TFP and me. I had just come from the health clinic and received bad news, I was not in a good mood, but I was being nice.

"Hey, I'm planning to make a short film, would you want to act in my film? Help me out?" I asked.

Jeff was trying to think about it.

"It is for my assignment," I then explained.

"Yeah, sure, okay," he answered.

His girlfriend popped up out of nowhere. She wondered what was going on. In my mind, I was thinking about the situation with Savannah, Jay, and me all over again. Maryilynn had long blonde hair and was overweight, she looked different than the picture I saw on Jeff's nightstand.

He introduced me to her. "This is my friend, Nabila."

I went on to class. I didn't think anything of it.

***

The next day, I visited the career center to see if I could get an internship. The career center was located on the first floor of Hall Memorial. The career advisor assisted me with my resume and then helped me get an internship with B.E.T.

While I was driving my red Ford Escort to B.E.T
to do the interview there, I listened to the song *"Tonight is
the Night"* sung by Betty Wright, on the radio. I wore my
wig and a brand-new brown office suit and shoes, with a
little makeup on my face. Looked at the map each time I
stopped at the traffic red light. B.E.T. was five miles away
from Gallaudet. I drove west on Florida Avenue. Took a
right onto Brentwood Parkway/ Ninth Avenue, heading
north. Turned right onto W Street. It wasn't too hard at
all.

I parked the car, got out, and walked up to the
guard at the gate.

"How do I enter the building? I asked.

"What is the reason?" he asked.

"I need to do an interview," I answered.

He asked me for my name.

"Nabila Geron," I said.

He checked the list and created a nametag for me.

I entered the building and sat down at a table with
five people. A light brown-skinned black woman with
dreadlocks was sitting in the brown leather seat next to
me.

"What will you do in the next five years?" she
asked.

"I hope to be a filmmaker," I said.

I didn't think that they would hire me because of my criminal record. However, I gave it a try. I regretted what I did in the past and made a mistake. I didn't know there were so many opportunities available like this.

But since I couldn't change the past, I wanted to be a filmmaker because I could make my own movies and not have anyone do a background check on me. But I realized that I needed a lot of money to make a movie. I needed to be a white male with no health issues or disabilities because that was the only way people would want to work with me.

And I couldn't report Jeff to the cops for the night he forced himself on me, it will be like Jeff said, "Nobody will believe you."

I didn't remember when he said that. We were in the parked car in Gallaudet's parking garage.

"Nobody will believe you that we had sex together," were his exact words.

He didn't know about my criminal past, but he meant because of the way I looked and the way he looked. I was just an ugly black woman and he was a handsome man. It was true.

***

A few days later, in Gallaudet's parking lot, Jeff and I walked toward my car and I had to use the key to unlock the door on the passenger's side.

"Go in," I told him.

"Don't tell me what to do!" He yelled.

I sighed. We sat in the car and I cranked up the car.

"Can you stop by the grocery store?" he signed.

"Ok," I said.

We arrived at the store, I parked, and he grabbed the cart.

"You can put anything in the cart, I'll pay for it," he said.

I smiled. I got my favorite frozen pizza.

We stood in line and he pointed. "Look!"

An obese Black female child was taking off her shirt in front of him, trying to be sexy. I felt sorry for Jeff, I could imagine him going through that every day. Well, I had been treating Jeff as a human being, no different from anybody. Because I was used to being around handsome guys, especially my father, who was a light-skinned handsome man.

***

After grocery shopping, at Jeff's apartment, we were carrying grocery bags and riding on the elevator with a brown-skinned Black man.

He greeted. "Hi."

Jeff introduced me to him. "This is my friend, Nabila."

Then the black man looked at me shamefully.

"Where's Maryilynn?" he asked.

I took that as a rejection. I knew what he was thinking that Jeff was way out of my league. I did agree.

"She's at Gallaudet, in classes," Jeff answered.

Outside of his apartment, I filmed him running from me. I was acting like I was a stalker. The Gallaudet's VHS camcorder I borrowed, was a little heavy. After that, we went inside his apartment.

"I'm hungry, let me try your pizza," he signed.

He took out a baking pan and handed me the boxed frozen pizza. He sat on his bed, watching me. I took the pizza out of the box, unwrapped it, and placed it in the oven. Then I turned on the oven.

"Wrong! You're supposed to preheat the oven first," Jeff said.

Then I realized he was testing me on how well I could be a housewife.

We ate the pizza while watching TV as we sat at the end of the bed. I finished mine quickly. I sat behind Jeff, wrapped my legs around him, then started humping on his back and rubbing on his crotch.

"I'm eating!" he shouted.

So, I got up and sat next to him.

"We can do a quickie after I finished eating," he later said.

"Okay," I signed.

He brushed his teeth. I thought about the condom, but I knew he wouldn't put it on.

"I'm ready, now," he said.

We took off our clothes.

"I'm fat," I told him.

"No, you look okay."

"Can I get on top of you?" I asked him

"Yes."

He laid on his back on the bed, which was covered with a white sheet, and I got on top. He slid his penis inside of my vagina carefully, because I was still kinda tight. I didn't know what I was doing, so I banged against him and hurt myself. He tilted his head back as if he was feeling so good, and then he got on top of me and fucked me. Then he cummed and spilled his sperm onto my tummy.

We got up and put our clothes back on. I was flirting with him again by sitting on his lap.

"I'm not leaving her for you. This muscle isn't for you, I work out because of my cerebral palsy," he snapped.

I didn't say anything. All I did was smile. There was no dialogue or anything that would make him say that to me. He thought he could read my mind.

"You can leave now," he then said.

***

Later, I was putting together the film that I shot of Jeff and I acting. In the editing room, I put the VHS tape into the VCR and used a 1990s editing machine. It was before the Final Cut Pro came out. It wasn't difficult to learn how to edit the video. I just had to be a perfectionist and have patience. I spent a couple of hours in the editing room, cutting some video scenes, telling the story, replaying, and then exporting the final video. I fell in love with making films.

***

The next day, Jeff was again blocking my path to the TFP department. He had a girlfriend and I didn't know what he wanted from me.

A young black woman dressed in short shorts with a string tank top walked pass by us.

"I want you to dress like that," Jeff demanded.

I thought that he didn't want to be treated that way. Oh, I forgot, he was a man, men like that. And I thought women didn't want to be viewed as a sex object. If women are dressing like that, why did they hate men touching them? They would yell out, "rape!"

"No," I said.

"I want you to work hard for me," he signed and spoke at the same.

"No," I said.

"You stupid, idiot! Look at me!" he yelled.

He showed off his beauty as if to say, "look at my hair, my good look, and body." Yeah, he was so attractive. But I didn't like his personality. I didn't want children, plus he was out of my league. I guess he had never met a girl like me who wouldn't compliment him on his appearance. So, I just left him and walked toward the TFP department.

***

In my dorm, I was sitting on the chair, watching TV at 9:00 p.m. My small gray Magnavox TV set was on the nightstand. I was hungry. There was a sandwich shop at the Student Academic Center that was open from 7:00 p.m. to 11:00 p.m. I really loved those grilled chicken sandwiches with lettuce, tomato, and mayo. I decided to walk over and get one.

Walked on the sidewalk from the Benson Hall, on a cool night. Entering the SAC building, I heard loud music coming from the sandwich shop. Once I entered the sandwich shop, I saw some people were dancing and some were sitting around. The security shutter was rolled down on the window counter. I saw Jeff standing at the portable bar with a few stools, near a brunette white woman who was dressed in a mini dress with her crossed bare pretty legs. They turned the sandwich shop into a nightclub.

I don't drink alcohol. I don't do nightclubs. It isn't my type of lifestyle. I spoke to Jeff and waved hi. He continued chatting with the brunette woman, she wasn't Maryilynn. I watched the people dancing toward the music. Some of them were deaf, but it seemed like they were having a good time. So, I left the sandwich shop and went to the mailroom. There was a letter from B.E.T. I opened it up and read it. "You are accepted at B.E.T. Internship."

***

During the summer semester in 1997, I had to stay at the Cleric Hall Dorm. It was a nice dorm, with two bedrooms and a shared bathroom. Every weekday, I woke up, got dressed up, and drove to B.E.T. I received my nametag from the security guard and did some office work. Then I went downstairs to the studios, sat at the table, shook hands with Lou Rawls, listened to the jazz musicians playing music. I didn't really like the internship, it was boring. I didn't like Jazz music.

I saw one of the B.E.T. Hosts, Sherry Carter, she was very beautiful. One of the job interviewers, the one with the dreadlocks, led me to the job board.

"Just pick one of these jobs and I can place you in that position."

I didn't want to work at B.E.T., working at the office. I was only interested in being a film director, plus I had a criminal record.

***

At night, in my dorm room, I woke up from a nightmare. I just wanted Jeff out of my life. Sex with him wasn't good anyway. Plus, he had a girlfriend. I was sick of all the sneaking around.

In the morning, I drove to his apartment and arrived at his door. I listened to a female voice and Jeff's voice. I knocked on the door and he answered. I barged in.

"Jeff was bothering me, and I just want you to know that," I told Maryilynn.

I tried to grab her purse, but Maryilynn was holding on to her purse tightly. She rushed out the door and Jeff sat down on his bed with his head down. I left and smiled. That's was what he get for calling me a stupid idiot. I was hoping that he wouldn't ever bother me again. I knew that making him angry would strain our friendship. I knew that if I tried to talk to him, he would do anything to avoid me. No more Jeff, no more Byron, no more Jay. No competition. No comparing me to another girl. I was free! It was a new life for me! But I was wrong, I wish that I hadn't done that. I wish I had left Gallaudet instead.

***

The summer internship was over. Fall classes were starting. I had to move out of Cleric Hall to move back to the Benson Hall. A new dorm roommate moved in and then out. I sat on the chair's crest rail and watched TV that was set on the five-drawers' chest. And I was getting hungry.

I walked from Benson Hall to the Student Academic Center, hoping the night club was gone. The sandwich shop was back. I saw Marcus as a cashier at the counter, who I had tried to ask for sex. I ordered my favorite grilled chicken sandwich. Marcus looked up. I

looked back and Jeff was standing behind me. He looked
so angry.

I turned around. "I'm sorry."

He fled out of the sandwich shop and I followed
him.

"Don't talk to me!" he screamed.

Then he stormed out the door, I followed him
outside of the SAC and tried to calm him down.

I noticed hundreds of cigarette butts on the SAC
patio ground. When I was a child, playing alone as I
usually did, I would pretend I was a bus driver using a
long five-foot-long stick as a bus and avoiding the
cigarette butts laying on the ground as a train stop, stop
sign, or traffic light. I went around them. I was a kid with
imagination when I was playing alone. Like a kid
imagined a ghost or playing with a dollhouse. So, when I
was at Gallaudet and I was bored, I would step over the
cigarette butt. A Hispanic Gallaudet student noticed me
doing this. She probably told everyone at Gallaudet what
I was doing, using that to bully or petty me.

I wish I had known that people were this evil. I
would have never gone to college at all. Words are so
powerful and can spread around, destroying people's
lives. I should have stayed at home and done nothing

with my life. If the time machine was real, I would set it back to 1991 and avoid college, avoid pursuing anything.

"Can we be just friends?" I asked.

He placed his middle finger on my lips. He left and I didn't really care. I went back into the SAC. I proceeded to order my sandwich with a can of Coca-Cola, then walked back to the Benson Hall. I took the elevator, went to my room, sat back on the chair's crest rail, watched TV, and ate my sandwich.

***

It was a new day, entering in the television studio with a news desk and chairs, camera prompter, film lighting, and lighting stand. The TFP professor was a tall, old white Ed Murrow lookalike. He didn't know sign language, he would have a sign language interpreter around him. He told us we needed to do the demonstration shot of the apple on the table. He had Dylan on one camera and another student, Taylor, on the other camera. I was in the production control room with one of the TFP staff and the Ed Murrow-lookalike professor. There was a window next to the video monitors, and I was able to see Dylan at the camera. I waved at him to do the close-up of the apple. He zoomed in.

"That is a perfect shot," I told the staff.

The professor agreed. Then Dylan zoomed out. I entered the TV studio and signed to Dylan.

"No, zoom in."

"Okay," he said.

Then I went back to the production control room and Dylan, a tall blonde-haired deaf white dude, zoomed out again.

"He did it again," the staff signed.

So, I went back to the TV studio and argued with Dylan. I pushed him and pounded on his chest.

"Stop it!" I yelled.

"You don't know what you are doing!" Dylan yelled back.

"The professor said it was fine. I like that shot," I said.

Taylor butt in and took his side. He's gay, he should know better.

Dylan was deaf and Taylor was a deaf gay man. I wondered if they ever faced discrimination from people with no disability. It would seem like deaf and gay people would have empathy and work together with me in Hollywood.

***

In fall of 1997, I had a film class that was from 1:00 p.m. to 2:15 p.m. English class was from 2:00 p.m. to

3:00 p.m. I always had to leave early to get to the English class. Jeff sat on the floor in the hallway near the classroom. I had thought I wouldn't see him anymore, but I guess my plan didn't work out. I ignored him and entered the English class.

The English professor, Ms. Pia, warned me and my classmates.

"If you are late, I will close the door. Even if you are one minute late, you shall not come to class. The door will be closed at 2:00 p.m. according to the watch on my wrist."

Jeff's Hispanic best friend was in the class. I didn't know if it was his and Jeff's idea for the professor to be strict, or if Professor Pia was usually like this.

One day, I got up from the table in the film class, and the TFP professor was pissed at me.

"Why do you always leave so early?" he asked.

"Because I accidentally conflicted the English class time with the film class time," I told him.

The TFP professor had never given us an assignment or a test. All he did was sit in the chair at the round table. Us classmates were sitting at the table with him as he sat with his legs crossed, in a gray suit, a wannabe Ed Murrow, talking all day. I figured leaving fifteen minutes early from his class wouldn't hurt.

I rushed out of the class, which was in the Merrill Learning Center, and headed to the English class in Hall Memorial Building. The buildings were a few feet away. I entered the building and saw Ms. Pia was closing the door. As I was walking fast, I looked at my watch, "1:59", then looked up at the huge clock on the wall, "1:57". She quickly slammed the door. I opened the door and entered the room.

"Leave, please leave," Professor Pia said.

I sat down at the desk anyway.

"Okay, I will get the security," she said.

As she walked out of the classroom, I got up and slammed the door. The class laughed out loud. I didn't care about the consequence. I was so sick and tired of nonsense rules.

***

Later that evening, I felt so bad about what I did to Jeff, because I wasn't a sociopath. I walked down to the Benson Hall computer lab and emailed him, trying to explain why I did what I did.

"I'm sorry."

"Don't email me!" he replied.

***

Next day, I had seen him almost everywhere, but I just walked by. When I was heading to Spanish class at

Hall Memorial Building, he was standing there in the middle of the hallway. I ignored him. If I went up to him, he might get angry.

Later, I used the computer in the Benson Hall's computer lab.

"I'm sorry," I emailed him again.

I didn't know if he got my email. I thought he blocked it.

***

In Benson hall, as I was going up the stairs, I saw the shadow of a person. I assumed it must be him, stalking me. As I got on my floor, which was where my dorm room was located, I decided to find out who the person was. I went up the steps, and the shadow moved, so I decided to give up and back down to my floor level.

***

The next day, again, the same thing happened. I decided to chase after the shadow up the stairs, even with a meal I purchased from the cafeteria in my hand. The door was swinging on the seventh floor; I opened the door and stood in the hallway. There was Jeff. I dropped my meal that was in a Styrofoam container on the ground and charged up to him. He laughed. He rushed into his blonde-haired female friend's dorm room. She was Alex's ex-girlfriend. I barged in and pushed him. We wrestled at one another. The campus police came in to break us up.

"What is going on?" one of the campus police asked me.

"I'm just tired of him stalking me," I said.

"Well Jeff is in the lobby, so upset. We are trying to calm him down," she said.

I saw Chris for the first time since I tried to ask him for sex. He was being nosy. I came up to him and hugged him.

Chris consoled me. "Are you okay?"

"Yes," I signed.

I picked up my meal, which was still intact in the container, and went downstairs to my dorm room.

***

I received an email from the Office of Student Conduct, which was located at the Ely Center. I went to the Office of Student Conduct and saw a nice-looking white woman in her mid-thirties with brunette hair.

"Are you Nabila?"

"Yes," I answered.

She showed me copies of the email that I sent to Jeff and warned me not to send him any more email.

"Okay," I said.

At the T.F.P. department, I was called to the Ed Murrow lookalike professor's small office.

He was sitting behind the desk and I sat in front of him.

"I will have to remove you from the TFP department," he said.

"Why?" I asked.

"I just don't think you should major in T.F.P. classes."

"Well, those deaf students are playing football, do you think they will play NFL in the future?" I asked.

He paused.

"Well, you might as well tell all deaf men that they can't play football anymore," I said.

I believed Jeff has something to do with it.

I went to the Registrar's Office to see if I could change my major to computer science, but instead, I asked for the withdrawal form. I had to get a signature from the TFP professor who was my advisor and from other staff. I went back to his office and handed him the withdrawal form.

"Whoa, I said you need to change your major, not withdraw from Gallaudet," he seemed confused.

"Well, I saw that I needed to take a lot of classes for computer major, that will take me three years to finish that, so I might as well go back to LeMoyne Owen College, which I only have a few classes to take," I said.

He tried to talk me out of it.

"Just sign the paper!" I argued with him.

Then I went by the Ely Center, entering the Office of Student Conduct's door, and told the brunette woman to sign the paper.

"Why?" she asked.

"Why not?" I asked.

She signed the form. Professors of all five of my classes, including Ms. Pia, signed the withdrawal form because I was leaving in the middle of the semester without finishing my classes. I gave Ms. Pia an attitude by not saying thank you because I didn't have to worry about showing up her class on time.

It was still daytime, so I walked to my dorm, Benson Hall, and packed up my things in my dorm room. I loaded up the red 1997 Escort car with luggage and clothes. When I was finished, it was night-time. My car was parked across from the Ely Center, which was about two hundred feet away from Benson Hall, which is why I was out of breath, from walking back and forth, loading the car. I didn't take any breaks at all. I put the key in the ignition and started up the car. As I was about to leave the parking lot, I saw Jeff's tall, dark figure standing by the exterior light outside of Benson Hall. Jeff was watching me leave. I said it out loud to myself in the car.

"Bye!"

And never looked back.

I left because I felt a strong force energy blockage. I didn't want to be in the negative toxic environment. I couldn't be a film director if there are obstacles. Sometimes you have to listen to the Universe and just leave. I could always come back when things are less intense.

***

After I left Gallaudet, back to Memphis, relaxing at home on Don Street. I went outside to get the mail. I looked down and saw that someone had dump hundreds of cigarette butts underneath our mailbox on the street.

The only person from Gallaudet that knew my home address was Alex, who lived on Bonwood Street. Deidre and Chris wouldn't know where I lived, unless they asked someone like Savannah, Jay, or James.

I received an email from Jeff. "You bullshit me, I'll bullshit you."

I was so glad that I had left Gallaudet. I was so glad that I didn't marry Jeff, there was no telling what kind of marriage that would be. And going through a divorce with him would have been horrible.

Nabby

BLACK ENTERTAINMENT TELEVISION
INTERN POSITION

BET On Jazz: The Cable Jazz Channel is offering internships to eligible candidates for the period June 1, 1977 thru August 30, 1997. The internship is for **credit only, there is no compensation.** Interested candidates should send their resume along with a letter from the appropriate instructor outlining the course stipulation and number of credits they will receive to:

BET On Jazz, 2000 W Place, N.E., Washington, DC 20018
Attn: R. Tucker

Below is a general description of the typical duties associated with the intern position offered.

· Assist producers with logging and timing tapes in preparation for edit sessions

· Assist producers with completion of music cuesheets, respective formats and release forms

· Assist research associate in compilation of data for jazz database

· Assist in researching information on upcoming jazz events or programs

· Handling video dub request for record labels, artists and BET associates

· Retrieve and respond to Jazz hotline calls

· Other production related areas as assigned

The ideal candidate will be available 2 to 3 days a week for 3 to 4 hours per day

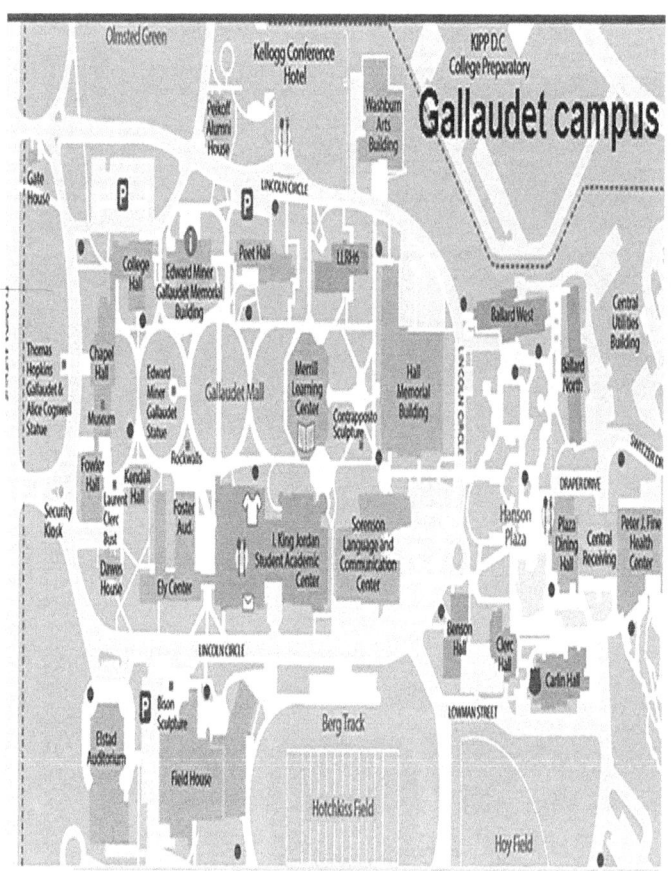

PURE

(timeframe: 1997 – 1999)

Dear Isa,

I re-enrolled at LeMoyne Owen College (LOC) in the spring semester of 1998. I went to Vocational Rehab. Tony was no longer my VR counselor. A bronze-skinned Black woman with glasses replaced him. I saw her at the church, World Overcomers on Winchester Road. I needed some help, so I asked her for a sign language interpreter.

"You will have to contact LeMoyne Owen College and have them pay for interpreter service," she advised me.

I went over to the LOC campus to the Administrative office in Brownlee Hall, and the staff didn't know how to get an interpreter.

I went home and looked online. I saw Deaf Connect of the Mid-South and I copied down the address. I drove to 6045 Shelby Oaks Drive in Memphis and requested the American Sign Language (ASL) interpreter. I should have known about it when I was first a student at LOC when I was having problems. If Tony wasn't such a stubborn person, I would not have gone to Job Corps and Gallaudet. I guess things happened for a reason.

***

There was no Byron at LOC anymore. I was going to the accounting class with an ASL interpreter. The interpreter asked someone to take notes for me. Pierre volunteered. He was a bald, kinda light-skinned Black. I sat next to him while I was looking at the interpreter. I understood accounting very clearly, and I was passing the class.

***

In physical education class at the C. Arthur Bruce/ Jerry C. Johnson Hall, I had to buy a tennis racket and wear a gym outfit. I was twenty-seven years old and badly out of shape. I never could do the one mile run around the gym track. I ran until the side of my stomach began to hurt.

***

I took a music class. I don't know what I was learning there. I don't remember if I was learning how to sing or learning how to play musical instruments. All I remember is that an English professor, a Black woman with hazelnut-colored skin-tone wearing glasses and a curly shoulder-length wig, waited for me to exit the class.

"Nabila, may I see you in my office?" she asked.

The office was next to the music classroom in Brownlee Hall.

"Yes, okay," I answered.

She sat down at her desk in a small office with no window. A lot of papers, files, and books clustered her desk. I sat on the chair opposite her.

"I'm writing a book about the cleft palate," she said.

I was puzzled. "Oh okay."

"Do you have cleft palate?" she asked.

"No, just Treacher Collins syndrome," I answered.

I didn't know why she would write a book about something she didn't understand. She needed to see someone like Joaquin Phoenix and asked him because he had a cleft palate. I wasn't sure if I had TCS.

A few months ago, I told the Treacher Collins Syndrome group on Yahoo that I may not have TCS because the genetic doctor at Gallaudet said I didn't have TCS or a Cleft Palate either. I was a "new mutant."

"Yes, you do have TCS!" they messaged me.

I guess they knew more than the doctors.

***

Later, I saw my high school ASL interpreter, Mrs. Haug in the statistics classroom. Mrs. Haug had shoulder-length blonde hair and looked a little bit like Barbara Walters.

"Let's go to the vending machine down the hallway," she signed before the class started.

"Why, what for?" I asked.

She didn't answer.

"Come with me," She signed.

We walked down the hallway of Gibson-Orgill Mathematics and Science Learning Center (GOMASL) to the vending machine. Mrs. Haug used her change to buy a can of Coca-Cola.

"Give this to your notetaker."

We walked back to the class, and I gave the drink to Pierre.

"As a thank-you gift," I told him.

"You didn't have to do that, but thank you," he was surprised.

***

After class, I went to my car in the parking lot, next to the GOMASL building, and my dad walked up with his cane.

"Hey, Dad! What are you doing here?"

"Well, I live near here, so I thought about visiting you," he answered.

"You want me to take you home?" I asked.

"Yeah," he answered.

We got to the house.

"I made some dinner, do you want to come in and eat?" he asked.

I almost hesitated.

"Yeah, okay," I replied.

We walked up to the house and a woman opened the door. I forget her name, but she was an okay-looking caramel-skin-toned Black woman with glasses. She welcomed us in. I don't clearly remember the meal. I believe it was sour cream, greens, and pork chops. It wasn't my dad's house. It was the woman's house. A beautiful-looking home almost looked like the one on Don Street. We didn't eat at the table. Just on the TV trays, watching TV. My dad used to be light-skinned, but I guess he suntanned by picking cotton and working on the farm, and his skin became brownish. He was still handsome-looking. I didn't understand why he never remarried or had more kids.

***

The next day, I was on my way to the accounting class, greeting my stepsister Shauna, near the stairway. I didn't ask what she was majoring in. We didn't really have a real good conversation.

A brown-skinned Black woman came up to me. "Hey, can I borrow your book? I want to make a copy of the book. The bookstore ran out of Accounting book."

I handed her the book. Shauna was standing there in the hallway of the GOMASL building with a copper-skin-toned man, watching me.

"I will give it back to you," the woman said.

"Can I come with you?" I asked.

"No, no, I'll give the book back to you," she answered.

She left out the door with my book, which was worth about fifty dollars. As I walked up the stairs, my gut feeling was telling me to go get my book. I went outside and followed the woman. She was heading toward the Alma C. Hanson Student Center.

The woman turned around. "I said I will return the book to you."

"No, I will go with you," I smiled.

She gave me back the book and left frustrated. I entered the GOMASL building and smiled at Shauna, who looked horrified. I guess she learned from me that someone could steal from you.

"I got my book back, whew!" I told her.

Shauna didn't say anything.

***

During accounting, I noticed Pierre's fingernails. He had a habit of biting his fingernails, damaging the nail, cuticle, and surrounding skin. He took great notes, but his fingernails were gross. He wasn't cute, just average-looking and bald. I gave him the duplicate papers so we wouldn't have to use the copy machine. I asked him if he wanted anything, such as a drink or whatever to show my gratitude for being my notetaker.

"No, thanks, I'll do it for free," he said.

***

In the study hall at the GOMASL building, I would usually sit there to study during the lunch break. I got up, gathered my stuff, and was heading to the next class. I walked by two Black women who were seated at another table.

"Are you okay?" one of the women asked.

I snapped back. "Yes. Are you okay?"

Her ignorant self didn't say anything. If you see someone who is different, don't be rude. Just ask, how are you?

After the statistic class, a person with a brownish skin tone, who was as short as me, walked toward me. I usually passed by him in the hallway in the GOMASL building.

"Are you okay?" he mimicked me with an attitude.

One day, I was in the advisor's room, the same advisor who helped me withdraw from LOC. I was at the table with her, discussing which classes I could take for spring semester of 1999. The guy who mimicked me came in and sat at the table with us. He chatted with her and then looked at me.

"How is your wife?" the advisor asked him while smirking.

He got up and left the room. I didn't see him anymore after that.

***

I passed the classes with the help of the ASL interpreters and notetaker Pierre. I felt like I wouldn't have passed the courses without their help. He was way better than Jeff. At home, in the dining room, with the IBM computer on Joe's brown wood dining table, I checked my email and decided to email Jeff.

"Nah, I got a new man, now," I emailed Jeff.

I was being childish. We argued back and forth over email.

***

In the spring of 1999, I felt that I didn't need the ASL interpreter for the business law class, since I had Pierre. All throughout the spring semester, it was the same routine for me—I was driving the red Escort, listening to Brandy's "*Never Say Never*" tape, singing along, and parking the car near the Brownlee Hall building. And climbing up the stairs and then sitting next to Pierre in the Business Law class.

One day, I was running late, and I saw one of my cousins. He was speaking so low, and I couldn't hear him at all.

"Hey, I need to go, I'll be late for my class," I said.

It was good to see a family member from my father's side to go to college.

***

I ran into Byron's brother, Brook, who looked very similar to Byron. But he had amputated legs. He was in a motorcycle accident. He was trapped underneath an eighteen-wheeler truck on the interstate. He was having a difficult time climbing the stairs. Brownlee Hall building was built in the 1930s, so there was no elevator. The only building that had the elevator was the Gibson-Orgill Mathematics and Science Learning Center (GOMASL).

"Do you want me to help you?" I asked.

"No. I got it," Brooks answered.

He climbed slowly upstairs, painfully. He had so much pride. That was the last time I saw him. I later heard that he died from an overdose of pain medicine.

***

In the GOMASL building, where the Division of Business and Economic Development office was located. I was visiting Mr. McFarland. He seemed like he was in charge of the division. He was at his desk, and there was someone already in the room with him; she was my classmate in the Business Law class.

"I need the degree to get this job. I got a kid at home who I have to feed," she whined.

I joined in. "Yeah, we don't need to take all of the minor classes such as physical education, English, and all that. I have been in colleges since 1991 on and off."

McFarland got up from his desk and headed toward the receptionist's room. He made a phone call. We waited a few minutes before coming back.

"You guys can graduate at the end of this semester."

Then he went back to the receptionist's office and made another call. My classmate and I high-fived. I wasn't expecting it. I was so surprised. Wow! I rushed home to tell my mom the news.

"Hey, I'm gonna graduate at the end of the semester!"

She seemed surprised. "Oh, really?"

"Yeah, my classmate and I were complaining to Mr. McFarland, and he said he will let us graduate!!!" I explained.

***

In Business Law class, I entered the room and noticed Pierre sitting in the back row. I went in the back and tried to sit next to him.

"No. I'm not writing notes for you anymore," he said.

"Well, I need to pass this class to graduate," I thought to myself. Maybe I need to buy him a can of Coca-Cola or something. Maybe I didn't thank him enough, or maybe Jeff got someone spying on me and told Pierre about me. Perhaps he just didn't want to help me graduate. I didn't understand. So, I sat in the front row of the class. The law degree professor who was a nice-looking, light-brown- skin-toned Black was showing concern. I didn't have an ASL interpreter. I just turned the hearing aid up really high and asked other classmates if I could copy off of their notes.

After the class was over, I followed Pierre all the way to his white pickup truck, which was parked on Walker Avenue, and grinned because I wanted him to tell me what was going on. He entered his truck and drove away. I knew he lived somewhere in Mississippi, but I forgot what city he lived in.

***

I walked back on the LOC campus and went to the GOMASL building to visit one of my professors who taught the economic class. He was overweight, about three hundred pounds, a white male, about fifty years old. I sat next to his desk in the chair, and he was sitting in front of the desk. I gave him the graduation clearance form to sign. He put his hand on my knee and saw I did not react. Then he signed the form.

***

At home on Don Street, I kept all the notes that Pierre had written and studied them. I re-read the business law book to memorize everything. And reviewed the new notes I had copied from other students. I studied every day.

***

A week later, I went to Business Law class, sat at the front row, ignored Pierre, and did the final test. The questions weren't that hard. I finished them, turned the test in, greeted the professor, and finally left the room. Whew! It felt like people's eyes were watching me.

***

At home, I ordered the college class ring online, had it engraved with 1999 on one side, BBA on the other side, and my name on the inside next to the word 10K, with a small diamond on top. Then I ordered my gown, cap, and LeMoyne Owen College scarf, which was purple with yellow words on it. I allowed my mom to do all of the graduation invitations.

***

A few days later, in my business law class, I sat alone in the front row. The professor gave me my test paper. She announced to my classmates that I made an A.

My classmates probably thought that I cheated by looking at Pierre's test papers all semester. But I guess they knew now that I am smart, too.

***

It seemed like everybody at LeMoyne Owen College was graduating. We were standing in line, marching toward the church pews, I didn't see Pierre. We sat in our assigned seats, while my mother and others sat on the pews on the upper floor. We listened to the speakers at the church podium, and our names were called out afterward. We were each given rolled papers by LOC staff. It was the best day ever. After graduation, we went to the back of the church. I don't remember well, but I couldn't find my mother and the others my mom invited.

That's when I saw Pierre for the last time. I didn't know whether he would ignore me or walk the other way, but he gave me a hug, and I thanked him for helping me as a notetaker.

Nabby

BOBBY DOUSE

(timeframe: 1999 – 2000)

Dear Isa,

I applied for a job at Kellogg, International Paper, and other places in Memphis. The only place that offered me a job was the Goodwill store, but I didn't want to be a cashier again. I had been a cashier for Kmart, and I had communication issues, especially with some people who wouldn't speak louder.

***

My mom, nephew, Aunt Mary, Jasmine, Alexis, and I went to Disney World in Orlando, Florida, in the summer of 1999. My nephew and Alexis were three years old, and Jasmine was eight. Jasmine was Aunt Mary's granddaughter, and Alexis was her great-granddaughter. All of them had skin the same color as mine. My mom and Aunt Mary were sisters. We drove there because we couldn't afford the airline ticket, though we could still afford our hotel rooms. I really did enjoy Disney World and wanted to work there. After the vacation was over, we all went back home to Memphis.

***

A few weeks later, I drove my red Ford Escort to Florida. I was so tired of driving. I wanted to go to the University of Florida in Gainesville because it was closer to Disney World. But as I was driving, I kept seeing the signs for Florida State University, which was in Tallahassee, along the interstate.

I applied to FSU in the fall of 1999, because I saw how nice the FSU campus looks. Later, I was accepted at FSU. I had my dorm room, and I enrolled in classes with my advisor at the FSU Student Disability Resource Center. They provided an ASL interpreter for me.

***

I lived in one of the ugliest dorms. I was on the twelfth floor. There, I met Bobby. He lived on the same floor as I did, right across from my dorm room. He always had his door open while he was checking papers. He was an assistant professor at Florida Agricultural and Mechanical (FAMU), where he taught history. FAMU was one of the historically black colleges and universities (HBCUs).

I didn't know why Bobby was staying at a dorm. I didn't know what other professors and assistant professors' living arrangements were. Maybe Bobby couldn't afford a house or an apartment. I guessed he liked staying in the dorm.

***

Bobby invited me to watch him teach a history class at FAMU. I sat at a desk with the other students, while he stood up front with the whiteboard behind him. He was nervous, and his body was noticeably trembling.

"How well did I do?" he asked me after the class. I lied. "You did okay."

***

I was majoring in motion picture arts. I didn't realize that FSU was one of the toughest schools in the country. I really didn't learn anything. I was in a film class where we watched *"Citizen Kane"*, directed by Orson Welles. We also watched the 1996 and 1968 versions of the *"Romeo and Juliet"* movies to compare them. I really liked the 1968 version. At the time, I really just wanted to be an intern at Disney World. I didn't want to learn anything.

***

After class, walking back to my dorm, I saw Byron and waved hello. He was with a dark-skinned Black woman. I didn't remember the conversation. He and the woman entered the elevator. I knew he had gone to FSU after he graduated from LOC. I didn't know what he was thinking when he saw me.

***

My roommates moved out, so I had the whole dorm room to myself. Bobby had his whole dorm room to himself, as well.

"Can you come in?" Bobby asked.

He always had his door wide open. I walked in his dorm room, and that was the worst decision I ever made. I sat next to him at the table, in an armless chair. The dorm room, a small apartment really, had a kitchen, a bathroom, and a living room. The kitchen had a stove, cabinet, and refrigerator. Gallaudet didn't have those things in its rooms, just the bedroom, living room, and bathroom.

Bobby was bald-headed and older, thirty-five years old. I was twenty-eight. Our skin color and complexion were about the same, though he was unattractive. I thought he would be more like Pierre, but I never knew Pierre that well, just as a note-taker.

"Do you want to come to church with me?" Bobby asked.

"Yeah, I can give you a ride there," I said.

***

On Sunday, I was feeling so depressed that I lie in bed all morning, thinking about Jeff and Pierre. There was a loud knock on the door. I ignored it. Then another knock, but I refused to get up. The knocking changed to banging, but I ignored that, too. I should have gone back home to Memphis. It was noon before I got up from my bed. I opened the door and crossed the hallway.

"What time is the church?" I asked, playing dumb.

"I was knocking on your door! Many times!"
Bobby said.

I apologized.

***

The next Sunday, I went to church with Bobby. It was nice. He introduced me to his church friends. The church was small with many black people there. I couldn't hear some of the things the pastor said, and I tried not to fall asleep sitting in the pew. I did enjoy the church choir, though.

***

In my film class, ASL interpreter was a blonde-haired white woman. She said she was from Tampa. The professor was about seventy, and he complained about Winona Ryder's acting. He also mentioned a test and when the test would be, so I made small copies of the book and stuffed them inside my shoes. People with disabilities can take tests in a small room in the Disability Resource Center. When I saw there were no surveillance cameras in the test room, I took off my shoe and took out the pages of the book. I looked up each question in the copies and found the answer before filling in the answer bubbles on the test.

***

A few days later, the film professor returned our tests. I got a B. I knew it was wrong to cheat, but I was thinking about the Disney World internship. I hadn't been to the Career Center at FSU, yet.

***

Later, I was sitting in Bobby's dorm room, he didn't say anything. He stood next to his bedroom door, inviting me in.

"Give me thirty dollars," he then said.

I got up, went to my dorm room, and retrieved the money. I also grabbed a condom out of my luggage that was on the dresser, then I walked back to Bobby's dorm room. I handed him the money and the condom. We went into his bedroom, which had two twin-size beds, a desk, a chest, and a closet. He took off his clothes and I took off mine. I laid next to him, watching him massaged his penis with lotion. "I hope he is experienced," I thought.

"You can get on top," he said.

He didn't want to use the condom. I got on top of him, and he pushed his penis inside my vagina. His penis wasn't normal. It was more like a boomerang shape, curved on the side. It felt like the cylinders were broken. The sex lasted a few minutes. Of course, I didn't have an orgasm. It was sad. I have had sex with three men, four times, but I have never orgasmed with any of them.

***

After that, it seemed like every day, he asked me for money. I got frustrated.

"Why do you always ask me for money? Give me back the money that you owe me!" I demanded.

He rosed from his chair, then went into his bedroom and came back out into the living room. I was still sitting at the table. He dumped a pile of papers on the table.

"See! I got bills. Plus, I am going through a divorce! I have no food in the refrigerator," he said.

The song *"Bills Bills Bills"*, sung by Destiny's Child, played over and over again on my CD player, every day while I was in my dorm room. I should have listened to Beyonce's advice: if a man is poor then dump him.

"That isn't my problem," I told him. "You need to get another job! Or get a better job than that stupid professor's assistant job that you have!"

I got up from the table and tried to push myself into his bedroom. He pushed me back and I tried again. He picked me up and threw me across the hallway. I slammed down on the hard floor. I quickly got back up.

"Give me back my money!" I yelled.

He threw a glass of water on me, then slammed his door. I got a whole egg from my refrigerator in my dorm room and threw it at his door.

***

A few weeks later, he was standing at the window in the dorm's twelfth-floor lobby, high on drugs. His eyes glazed over, and he was sweating profusely. I walked over and stood next to him. I was a caring person. I had never seen a person overdose, that just gave me another reason to not be with men anymore.

"Stay with me for a few minutes," he said.

I rubbed his back. I knew Bobby had taken the pills from the brown bottle, because he told me he had to pick up a prescription from some guy he met on a sidewalk on FSU's campus, across from the dorm building. Bobby was buying illegal prescription drugs.

***

A few days later, I saw a mentally disabled white man sitting on the orange plastic couch in the living room of Bobby's dorm. He had a pen and a checkbook in his hand. Bobby slammed the door in my face. I wondered how many people he had asked for money.

***

The next day, someone knocked on my door and I opened it. Bobby was in his dorm room with the door wide open, sitting at the table, checking papers. I went across the hallway and sat next to him at the table.

"What?" I asked.

He asked me for more money. I got up and went back to my dorm room. I didn't give him anything. I wasn't sure if he was using my money to buy drugs.

***

Another day, he asked me if he could drive my car. He wanted to go gamble with his fraternity brothers.

"Okay," I said and gave him my car keys.

I could see why some people are mean because some people take advantage of nice people. I waited and waited for him to come back while lying on my bed, but I fell asleep.

I could never find a vibrating alarm clock for the deaf that could wake me up, I always had to sleep with my hearing aid to hear the regular alarm clock.

At 2:00 a.m., there was a knock on my door. It was Bobby. He handed me my car key, and I rushed outside to see if the car was okay. He followed me, but the car seemed fine.

Bobby had his own car — a light tan classic car from the 1960s. I remember he got pulled over by the campus cops for speeding. Bobby never told me he got a car. I did ask him, but he won't talk about it.

***

The next day, there was a knock on my door. As usual, I walked across the hall and into his dorm room, where I sat at the table next to him. He was opening his mail and pulled out a credit card from the envelope.

"Can you drop me off at the grocery store?" he asked.

"Okay," I said.

At the grocery store, Bobby had one hundred dollars worth of food in his cart, and Bobby gave the cashier his credit card after she scanned everything. While we waited for the charge to be approved, she bagged up the groceries and put them in the cart. The charge hadn't gone through yet, but it hadn't been declined either.

"Can we go? I don't know what is wrong with the machine, so can we go?" Bobby asked the cashier.

The cashier was confused and nodded yes. Bobby and I walked out of the store with the bagged groceries. I didn't think Bobby activated the card. I felt like Bobby had scammed the poor cashier. He scammed the store. He may have caused her to lose her job.

***

The fall semester ended, and the spring semester began. I was in another film class, but on the first day the ASL interpreter didn't show up. When I walked into the Disability Resource Center, the receptionist spoke without me having to ask anything.

"The ASL interpreter didn't show up because she was complaining about the low salary," she said.

"Oh," I responded.

"We will try to find another ASL interpreter for you," she added.

"Alright then," I said.

The receptionist was a very nice black woman with a toffee complexion, short hair with some curls, and a little overweight. I showed her the short story I had written for a class, and she loved it.

I fell in love with the creative writing class I had that semester. I wrote a short story, but I had a problem with my grammar. I blamed my elementary special ed teacher for poor teaching. I made some friends with my female classmates and the professor. They were white and friendly.

"I really like to watch Dr. Phil's show," the English, pale-skinned professor with brownish hair said.

"Yeah, Oprah helped him have a TV show," I told him.

***

Sinbad, the comedian, came to FSU. I visited the ticket office and purchased two tickets, then, headed back to my dorm.

I walked into Bobby's wide-open dorm room and showed them to him.

"I got two tickets."

"For what?" Bobby asked.

"Sinbad is here. We can go see him on stage at the FSU auditorium," I said.

"No, he's boring. He isn't funny," he said. The only places Bobby would go with me were his friend's house, the grocery store, Taco Bell, Blockbuster, the ATM machine, and the church. I hung out with Bobby because he didn't have a girlfriend, he wasn't perfect, he was ugly, the only friend I could talk to, he didn't judge me, he was nice, and we would go to some places.

I went alone, sold my other ticket to someone, and watched Sinbad. Bobby was right: Sinbad wasn't funny anymore. Sinbad was on the stage, and my seat was on the upper floor to the right of the stage. Sinbad stopped performing and ordered the light technician.

"Turn the lights on!"

The whole room lit up. He looked up and looked directly at me. That was when I realized how deformed my face was. I thought that I didn't look so bad. People kept telling me that I looked okay, but I really didn't believe them. The way Sinbad had to stop the show and stare at me made me feel like I must be a freak show.

***

The next day, I gave Bobby some more money. I allowed him to drive my car while I sat in the passenger seat. A car was pulled up on his side, and Bobby rolled down the window.

"Hey! Roll down your window," he yelled out the window.

The driver of the other car rolled down her window. Bobby balled up the twenty-dollar I gave him and tossed it into the driver's window.

"I told you that I would pay you back!" he laughed.

"That was one of the church members," he told me.

***

I went to the grocery store to buy some food and I heard the song, "*Don't come around here anymore*," sung by Tom Petty. I didn't know if they played the song all the time or if it was just for me. I guess that I was that ugly.

***

A few days later, Bobby knocked on my door and I got up. I answered the door and saw that he was across the hallway, sitting at the table in his room, checking papers as usual. I walked across the hallway and into his dorm room.

"Why don't we go on a long trip today, somewhere far away?" he asked.

"Okay," I said.

I went back to my dorm room and got my keys. I shuffled a deck of playing cards, which I used as tarot cards.

I asked a question. "Should I bring my debit card?"

I pulled up the king of spades. A king of spades represents an authoritative man who may create trouble.

While on the road, Bobby saw that the car was nearly out of gas. He pulled up to the gas station and parked the car near the gas pump.

"Give me your debit card," he said.

"I left it in my dorm room."

He got upset and sat back down in the car. While we were headed back to the dorm, he spat tobacco at me angrily. He was abusing me. I didn't understand why people hate me so much for hurting other people, but it was okay for them to hurt me. I was scorned for not being perfect, but nobody else was all that perfect either.

***

In my dorm room, I had a TTY, a teletypewriter for deaf people to use to make a phone call. I typed in Bobby's church's phone number and a staff member answered.

The relay operator relayed. "Hello?"

I typed in. "Tell other people not to give Bobby money. He has been asking everybody for money and even me."

"Okay, I'll let them know," The relay operator relayed.

I hung up the TTY after typing thank you.

Some people at the church were hypocrites. Bobby was a Christian, so he shouldn't have been acting like that toward someone who is unfortunate. All of this forgiveness and blah blah blah. That's why I turned to tarot cards and astrology, how dare people criticize me.

***

Later in the evening, I decided to call the police. I called 911 on the TTY.

"What is your emergency?" The 911 operator answered.

"It is a non-emergency. A man stole my money. He told me he would pay me back, but he never did," I answered.

I didn't know that spitting tobacco at me was an assault. I didn't know much about the law. If I had known, he would have gone to jail for doing that, especially since he was abusing a disabled person.

Moments later, the cops came by. They were two typical white male cops. They knocked on my door and I answered. I explained to them that he kept asking me for money and never paid me back. They knocked on Bobby's door and he opened the door. He showed them a note from me saying, "You don't have to pay me back."

"Don't give him any more money," the cops told me and then left.

At least it was on the record. If he bothered me again, I could call them again.

***

At the FSU library, there was a computer lab where I could get online and use Yahoo and other emails. I searched for Byron's email address and I found it.

"Are you still at FSU?" I emailed him.

A few minutes later, Byron responded. "Yes."

I was surprised by that. I thought he wouldn't respond at all. We continued to email each other. I saw Byron more than twice. I love to relive that moment, getting a hug and all.

I went back to the dorm, feeling so happy. I just wished that I hadn't had sex with Bobby. I wished that I hadn't befriended Bobby. I thought he was going to be my future husband. Since I didn't give Jeff a chance to know me, I decided to give some guy a chance, and it happened to be Bobby. I realized that men don't want me at all. I was just someone for them to pick on, and use. Bobby was a waste of my time. Instead, I should have gone to the Career Center, put all of my energy into that, and see if I can become an intern at Disney World.

***

When I got off the elevator on the twelfth floor, I saw that Bobby's door was wide open and all of his things had disappeared. Bobby moved out to another dorm room. I didn't know what dorm room.

I wanted to move, too, because I was tired of walking two miles to class every weekday. I thought the off-campus housing was much closer, but I still had to use my car to get to classes, and parking was always so difficult to find. I ended up getting a parking ticket for parking illegally in the handicap parking space. So, I moved out of the dorm and moved into the off-campus apartment.

***

In my creative writing class, I wrote a film script. That was something I knew how to do from Gallaudet. Two of my friendly white female classmates offered to meet me at the dorm that I moved out of to rehearse for my class project. I met them in the lobby, and we had so much fun, laughing and goofing around. Then, an elevator was opening, and Bobby stepped out, carrying a box. I ignored him. That was the last time I saw Bobby.

***

A few days later, I went to the International Program office. I should have gone to the career center to try to get into Disney World internship, but I didn't have to do it right away. I could always try to get into Disney World internship at the age sixty. I didn't have to do everything at the young age. Anyway, I saw International Program flyers on bulletin boards. So, I decided to visit the International Program office instead.

"Am I qualified to do this?" I asked the receptionist.

"What is your student ID number?" the receptionist asked.

I gave her my school ID over the four-foot wooden desk. The receptionist was a white, average-looking young woman. She was keying information into the computer.

"Uh, yeah, you are," she said.

I smiled. "Can I go to Paris, France?"

She smiled back. "Yeah, you can. Just fill out this form."

So, I filled out the application and submitted it to her.

"Great. We will contact you soon," she said.

"Okay, thank you."

***

I decided to move back to the dorm again. The off-campus apartment was too far from my classes. I was so tired of not being able to find a parking space to park my car. I went inside the dorm building and I asked for the same room.

"No, you will move in a different room and will have a roommate," the residence advisor said.

***

I moved into the dorm room, 1202 with Irene, a young, dark-skinned Black woman. I knew that she would give me a hard time because she wasn't happy having a roommate. I didn't know, I thought it was all planned by the residence advisors because nobody was living in my old dorm room, 1212. It didn't make sense to have me move to a room with a roommate.

At night, I slept on the bed that was next to the sliding window. Irene blasted her radio loudly at night while I had my hearing aid on. I had to wear my hearing aid so that I could hear the regular alarm clock. I still didn't have the Sonic Bomb vibration alarm clock that was designed for deaf people.

"Please turn that down," I told her.

She got up and left the dorm room. I knew she was going to get the campus police and the FSU staff. While she was gone, I scratched up her favorite CDs with a stapler and stacked them back together as an act of revenge.

I had to move out and back into my old dorm room, but I drove home to Memphis to stay for a few weeks to relax and recuperate. Then, I drove back to FSU and went back to my old dorm room, 1212. They had packed my stuff in a shopping cart. I didn't unpack anything because I found an envelope on the floor, near the door, as if someone slid it underneath. I opened the envelope and pulled out a letter. I read the letter, and it said, "Eviction, you have fifteen days to move out." I rolled the shopping cart out of the dorm room, entered the elevator, and put all of my things in my car. I drove back home to Memphis and never completed the spring semester. I didn't like FSU anyway, the parking sucked, the city was ugly, people sucked, the buildings were ulgy, and the classes were unnecessary.

***

I thought because Bobby and my three ex-roommates were working with Residential Advisors, Campus Police, and Housing staff. They got together because I wasn't getting along with my ex-roommates. And my ex-roommates wanted revenge.

All I did was rearrange the furniture in the bedroom because I didn't want to sleep next to the sliding window. When my first ex-roommate walked in, she didn't like that. She moved out.

The second ex-roommate moved in. She was grinding her teeth at night and I couldn't sleep as I was wearing a hearing aid to hear the regular alarm clock. I told her to move to another room.

I didn't want to deal with any more roommates, so I damaged the twin bed… the third ex-roommate had to find another dorm room to stay in.

I felt that the residential advisors and housing had handled my situation poorly. They should have allowed me to have the whole room by myself, instead of evicted me.

***

A few days later, when I was at home in Memphis, I realized I still had Bobby's number. I didn't use the TTY machine but used the regular phone instead. I dialed his number and held the phone up next to my bone conduction hearing aid.

He picked up. "Hello?"

I put the phone down to my mouth and screamed loudly in his ear, and then hung up. I laughed so hard, then I threw his phone number in the trash.

Nabby

FSU Disability Resource Center

Deaf alarm clock

COOLNOG

(timeframe: 2000)

Dear Isa,

I received a letter from the FSU International Programs. I thought it would be a rejection letter because I felt that people hate me. But I was accepted to go to Paris! I was so happy because when I was at Gallaudet, the Black male doctor at the Student Health Service wouldn't allow me to travel to Costa Rica because I had low blood anemia.

I used my student loan to pay for the dorm room and schooling in Paris. The only thing I had to pay for myself was the plane ticket. I did ask if I'd have a roommate and they said no, which was good because I didn't have to deal with a narcissist.

I picked Paris because people on TV always bragged about Paris. Paris was like BMW. I just wanted to see how wonderful it is. I really liked glamourous life and luxury stuff. I liked the feeling like I was wealthy. I wanted to do what the wealthy people do.

I packed my bags and had someone braid my hair. I was all ready to go, but my mom was late. She had to do some errands, and I didn't know why. She knew it was the day she had to take me to the airport. I called a taxi on the TTY. Eventually, my mom showed up, but I told her that the taxi was coming now.

It was getting late. Finally, the taxi came. The driver, who looked about sixty years old, a typical black male, helped me load my luggage and bags into the trunk.

On the way to Memphis International Airport, which was fourteen miles away, I kept looking at my watch. We arrived at the airport and I had to use a cart to carry my luggage and bags. I stood in the line at the ticketing area and the ticket agent called me up to the counter.

"May I have your confirmation number and ID please?"

I gave her the paper containing my flight details along with my ID.

"You've missed the flight to Atlanta. You will have to catch the next plane, to catch the plane that goes to Paris," she said.

"Okay," I said.

She was searching and searching, and I stood waiting and praying.

"Well, there are no more planes heading to Atlanta for you to catch," the agent said.

"I'll check the other airline's flight to see if they are going to Atlanta. Thank you," I said.

I went to Delta airline. They charged me a thousand dollars to fly with them. So, I wrote a check and gave it to them. They attached a tag to my luggage and bag. Then I finally got on the plane, and I hoped that I would make it to catch the flight in Atlanta to go to Paris.

I finally flew to Atlanta, and I hurried to get to the gate. I finally reached the gate. And the American Airline staff said I missed that flight.

"There is another plane that will fly to Paris, but there is no available seat. You will have to be on standby," she said.

She set up the ticket and handed it to me, I sat in the lounge and waited for someone to not show up. I doubted that I would get to Paris. I looked around. Atlanta airport was nicer than the Memphis airport.

Surprisingly, American Airline staff called me up! And finally, I was on my way to Paris! Finally, on the plane, I sat by the window, next to a brunette white man in a business suit who had the aisle seat. The white couple sitting behind me kept dropping their tray over and over and over again, nonstop for the whole seven-hour trip. I forced myself to be passive. I guessed they were a few of my enemies from FSU and Gallaudet. If I wasn't so passive, I would have gotten up and beaten the shit out of them. But I chose to ignore them. Sometimes they stopped when they were tired. "Well, good," I thought.

I had to use the restroom, so I got up and left my return flight ticket on the seat. When I returned back to my seat, the ticket was gone.

"Watch, she will panic and say oh my God where is my ticket?!" a female voice from behind.

Of course, no, I didn't do that. I didn't panic or say anything. I decided to stay passive. They continued to drop the tray table, but there was no reaction from me. If I did react to it, the airline would probably turn the plane around and go back to Atlanta to tell me to get off the plane for bad behavior. I guessed that is what their intentions were. They didn't want me to go to Paris.

I didn't complain to the flight attendants because I didn't care. I believed the other passengers didn't care about the noise.

Finally, we landed. "So cool," I thought. The couple and I were the last people to get off the plane. I stood up from my seat. The couple got up from their seats and walked down the aisle slowly. They were staring at me with angry look on their faces. I didn't say anything. I just watched them leave. Why would I want to argue with them? Are they friends of Jeff or one of my ex-roommates? I rather move on.

***

I walked down to the Paris airport's baggage claim area and saw someone held up the sign "FSU International Programs", and I got on the bus to the Paris University dormitories. I had my own room, no roommate, but no private bathroom or kitchen, just the bed, drawers, and a window. I had to use the gender-neutral restrooms with the showers. The gender-neutral didn't bother me one bit, no men want me anyway.

***

The study abroad classes weren't at the University of Paris. I had to walk across the street to the metro station and catch one of those trains to get to my classes. I had to walk a long distance and go into one of those old buildings.

I was in the classroom with a green board, about fifteen student desks, and a professor's desk, but there was no ASL interpreter. I couldn't hear much, and just looking at the white male professor who seemed to be middle age with dark hair, I had no idea what he was lecturing about. I didn't care. Paris was the reason I was here.

At the end of the class, Kunal, a short male, almost handsome, Indian, with nicely trimmed black hair, wanted to walk with me to the dorms. He was the only man that I got to go sightseeing with him every day. He was the only man who introduced me to new food like mussels, crepes, and lamb gyros.

***

One day, I looked at my reflection in a restaurant's mirrors and I looked so ugly.

"What's wrong?" Kunal asked.

"Nothing," I answered.

I kept forgetting what I looked like. I wished I was pretty. That really ruined my fun. Every time I looked in the mirror, I wanted something surgically done on my face, maybe some silicone in the cheeks. My long, braided hair covered up my small ears, but that didn't help completely. I didn't know why Kunal was even hanging out with me.

***

A week later, I used one of Gallaudet's old 1960s Canon cameras on the bus trip to the Paris dungeon with the FSU students, but it only took black and white pictures. I forgot to return the camera back to Gallaudet when I borrowed it in 1997, but since I still had it, I decided to bring it to Paris. I was sitting next to an overweight, blonde-haired, young White woman on the bus, on our way to the Paris dungeon. I was almost asleep when the woman opened up the camera's back cover. I should have punched her in the mouth, but I decided again to be passive. My roll of film was ruined, so I didn't have any pictures to prove to the world that I was in Paris. Next time I go to Paris, I'll take a selfie camera. It was the year 2000, so I didn't have a cell phone.

***

One day, I decided to walk to the Champs-Élysées. As I left my dorm, the mean white girl with brown hair, five feet tall, was smoking with the other brown-haired young white woman. They were smoking on the porch. They planted thirty cigarette butts all over the three-step porch. Maybe Jeff and his friends were behind this, having someone else do his dirty work, taking revenge on me.

I didn't know it would take so long to get there while walking on foot from the University of Paris to the Arc de Triomphe. It was daylight when I started walking and when I finally got near the Arc de Triomphe, it was night. I wasn't sure how to get across the street, because the cars kept going round and round the monument. There was no walk sign or traffic light. I ended up running across, despise it being nighttime so the cars couldn't see me at all. I finally made it into the Arc de Triomphe. I looked at some pictures and writing on the wall for a few minutes, but when the security guard saw me, he shut off the light.

"We're closed!"

So, I walked back down the steps and ran across the street as the cars honked at me and I almost got hit.

On my way back to the dorm, I got lost, but, luckily, I had a map. It took me four hours to get back, but I returned at 3:00 a.m. My legs were cramping from so much walking. The next time I go back to Paris, I will rent a car to drive around because the distance between the landmarks made them too difficult to walk to.

***

The FSU International Programs did provide a shuttle bus for students to go to some sightseeing with the leader. The leader was a white American man, average-sized, and about sixty-five years old. One day, he wanted to talk to me after he heard that my father passed away from a heart attack.

"Do you want to fly back home?" he asked me.

"No, I think he would want me to stay in Paris. He's here in spirit," I answered.

My father was sixty years old. Why did he have to die while I was in Paris? I didn't understand why he had never gotten his life on track. I helped him get Social Security Income. I didn't understand why I had to bring him the government check. He figured out how to get his SSI check sent to his mailbox. My dad had an apartment.

He was no longer living in somebody's house, not leeching off of anybody. Then he messed that up, got put out of the apartment, and ended up in the nursing home. My mother really made a bad decision in marrying my father and having kids with him. She didn't listen to her parents. And then she criticized how I lived my life!

***

While riding on the train with some friends and Kunal, a black woman—she looked African—gave me a card offering to braid my hair because my braids were fuzzy on top of my head. But I was so broke.

***

On the field trip to the wine valley outside of Paris when we were wine tasting, Kunal held the glass up, implying I should drink some more wine. I bought a bottle of red wine and we all got on the bus.

After I sat, I was singing "*Red Red Wine*" by UB40 and everyone was smiling. There were no black or young white men on the bus, most of the students were white females. There were three black women, including me. Kunal was the only young male on the bus. Our leader and sometimes my professors came along with their wives too, on these bus trips.

I didn't drink alcohol, but I bought the bottle of red wine for my mom, as well as a reddish urn, and a sculpture of the last supper with all twelve of the Black disciples and Jesus.

***

While I was in my dorm room, I did have to do homework, I hadn't read the books, so I just made things up in the essay. One of the professors would mark on the papers 'I don't understand!' but I didn't care.

***

I went down to the basement to wash my clothes and there I saw the overweight young white woman who messed up my film roll on the bus.

"How are you doing in class?" she asked.

"I don't know, I'm not here for classes, I just want to be in Paris," I answered.

She was about to leave the laundry room to tell everybody, but she could tell I didn't care. Gossipers are so evil.

"How do you like Paris so far?" she asked.

"I like it, cool place, I like castles and everything."

See, that is what life is like when you are passive. I just chilled out and didn't stress about anything. People like her have been around toxic people. She had been around negative energy. Stop all the hate. Forgive each other. Let's chill out and stop hurting one another. Let's have some fun. Think positive. Be around positivity.

***

In the dorm's kitchen, Kunal, a blonde-haired female, and I made spaghetti. We were sitting at the table.

"If you put some sugar on it, it will taste better," I told Kunal.

"Really? Let me try," Kunal said.

He sprinkled a little sugar on his and tasted it.

"Yum, it does taste better."

He turned and asked the blonde-haired girl if she wanted some sugar on hers, but she shook her head. The African security guard walked up to the kitchen door with his index finger on his lips.

"Shhh, residents need to sleep, you are too loud," he said.

He left. Kunal talked loudly again. The security guard came back. I was mimicking him.

"Shhhh," I said, with my index finger on my lips.

The security guard laughed loudly, waking up some people in the dorm.

***

The next day, I took a field trip to the Louvre with the FSU students. I didn't know there was so much stuff in Paris. There were so many paintings and statues displayed in the museum. Then I decided to enter a room that nobody else was in. I walked all the way to the back,

I tried to see the picture that was hiding back there in thick glass.

"Wow," I said about the picture of Mona Lisa, it was so astonishing.

It was the best painting I have ever seen.

***

The leader never took us to go see the Eiffel Tower, so I decided to go alone. I walked up the stairs and I was so out of breath, but I made it up to the top. The mean girl came over to me, and I guessed she was following Jeff or Bobby's orders to hurt me. She came over with another FSU student to talk to me. I didn't trust her. She was acting like she was going to hang out with me, but then she disappeared. I didn't bother to look for her. I wouldn't allow her to ruin my study abroad trip. So, I continued to enjoy my time at the Eiffel Tower, looking out at the high-rise view.

***

I didn't hang out with Kunal too much, because every time I was with a man, they always messed up my life. Pierre nearly messed up my chance to get a college degree from LOC, for example.

I decided to go on a boat ride with Kunal and a brunette female friend, who was a friend of the mean girl, on the Seine River. We rode on the top deck of the cruise, at night, watching the Eiffel Tower's light sparkling like champagne. I took pictures of the Eiffel Tower with a Fujifilm disposable 35mm camera. Paris was so beautiful. I could see why people love it so much. So, I got bad pictures of the Eiffel Tower at night, a picture of one of my favorite bridges over the Seine River, and a picture of Kunal in my possession.

***

Luckily, I saw Notre Dame before part of it burned recently. I didn't see any hunchback man, though. If I ever met him, I would tell him that it is okay to come out and hang out with people. He was disfigured, just like me. He would have had some hunchback surgery procedure if he was still alive today.

***

Next day, I skipped classes and rode the Eurostar train to London without telling anyone. My plan was to spend a day in London. I left early in the morning, it took about two and a half hours to travel from Paris to London.

I tried not to fall asleep so that I wouldn't miss hearing the speaker announcing that the train stopped in London.

The Eurostar train stopped about five times to drop off people or to pick people up. But I couldn't stay awake; I slept and woke myself up each time the train stopped. I was thinking, "Is this London?" I got up and saw "London" on the displayed sign outside. So, I got off quickly before the train's door slid shut.

The first thing I did was to catch a big red bus. I sat on the top deck. The tour guide understood my English. I guessed I spoke proper English while everyone else from the USA didn't. She looked like Mel B, as known as Scary Spice.

"Where is Queen Elizabeth?" I asked.

"She's in Scotland because many people are entering Buckingham Palace," she answered.

"Oh, people can go inside the palace?" I asked.

"Yeah, you have to go buy a ticket before you can enter the palace."

"Oh okay."

I didn't have much time, so I got off the bus, but couldn't find the palace. "Why would the Big Bus drop me off here?" I was wondering. I walked around and saw a taxi. I went up to the taxi driver who was overweight and White with a white buttoned shirt.

"Can you take me to Buckingham Palace?" I asked the taxi driver.

"Okay sure," the taxi driver said.

I was about to open the back door, but the taxi driver drove off.

Maybe he was being racist or just rude. Or he might have thought I was joking around. But he could have told me that the palace was over there, just a few feet away.

So, I checked the map and followed the map directions. And finally, I was at Buckingham Palace, crowded by people. I watched the men with red suits and tall black hats marching in front of the palace. Then I wondered why people were standing around. 'What are they waiting for?' I thought. Then I saw fifty men on horses trotting in the street and entering the palace gate. That was the coolest thing ever. I didn't expect that. So, I was trying to figure out how to enter Buckingham Palace. I asked one of the guards who was trying to keep people off the fence. People were squeezing against each other.

"How do I get inside that building?" I asked one of the guards.

"Go there and look for the sign," He pointed his finger.

I walked down the left side of the palace and saw the sign saying, "Tickets here". So, I bought a ticket and stood in line. Finally, I went in and did a quick tour. I saw art pictures on the walls, the throne, the garden, and the souvenir shop.

I didn't have much time to see everything in London. The Study Abroad semester was nearly over. It was time to get back on the Eurostar train and go back to Paris.

***

Next day, in Paris, I was in Kunal's room. We were just chatting with the brunette FSU girl, she was friends with the mean girl, the one who sat next to the mean girl on three-step porch, planting about thirty cigarette butts on the steps.

"I quit smoking," she said.

Kunal was cheering, and she was smiling. She had to leave the room.

"I'll be back."

She left me and Kunal alone in his room. I was sitting on the chair near the end of his bed. He was on his bed, lying on his back with his legs bent. He placed them so that my head seemed to be between his legs as if imagining me giving him a blow job.

***

The next day, the last day of the field trip, the leader said that we had to stay in a hostel for the night, which meant I had to stay with a roommate. My roommate was White and about my height with short brownish-blonde hair. I was letting her be the boss of me. I was being passive. I counted my change, it was about fifty-eight cents. I was waiting for my Social Security income to show up in my bank account. I kept my change in my purse. It was good that the field trip was paying for our meals.

At night, I took a shower and wetted up my braided hair. I went to sleep next to my roommate on our queen-size bed. I fell asleep on my back. A few hours later, she woke me up.

"You're snoring, turn on your side," she said.

So, I turned on my side and went back to sleep.

It was morning so I got up and got dressed up in my fresh clothes, I noticed the change in my purse was even less. So, I re-counted it was now thirty-eight cents. I knew it was the roommate, but I won't get mad over twenty cents. That meant I couldn't buy a bag of chips from the small store across from the dorm building in Paris after we get back from the field trip. I would starve until the Social Security income came in. I remained passive.

***

We took the bus and we headed to Amboise Castle. One of the professors was passing out tickets to everyone except me because I had decided to not go up to the castle with the group.

I walked out the castle and walked down the road, looking around—nothing but a dirt road. I turned around and walked into the parking area, got on the bus, and sat there for an hour, just relaxing. Later, I was bored. I decided to go to the castle. I hopped off the bus and walked toward the castle. Kunal saw me while he was with the FSU students, heading to the restaurant next to the castle. He waved at me. It seemed like the only thing restaurants in Paris served was baked chicken and wine.

I went up to the ticket counter to check whether I had any money on my debit card to purchase a ticket. The cash register approved my card. Woah! I had money now. So, I went up to the castle and gave myself a tour. Pictures, the interior-designed bedrooms, the throne, and everything else were lovely. After that, I went into the restaurant to join others.

***

On Bastille Day, I was hanging out with Kunal and some female friends. We were at the metro station, just standing around, waiting for the subway. The mean girl was talking to a nice blonde-haired young woman, and I was staring at the mean girl. I should never take my eyes off the enemy. There was no telling what she'd do next to be mean to me. While I was staring at the mean girl and looked at the middle-aged, overweight man, I saw he was very drunk, and probably could read my mind. He hopped off the short wall, walked toward her, put his hands on her arms, and shook her back and forth, flicking a cigarette at her and scorning her. This cheered me up. I was happy to see that, and nobody stepped in to help her.

***

Finally, the metro train arrived, and we got to the destination. We walked to the park, and we decided to sit on the short-walled fence. I was sitting next to the prettiest young White brunette woman, about five feet tall and thin—I forgot her name. She looked more like Amelia Heinle, the actress in The Young and the Restless. I didn't know where Kunal went, but I believed he was somewhere with us. We were watching the fireworks when a colorful LED glow light bracelet was thrown at us. The woman next to me thought it was a firecracker and panicked.

"Oh shit!" she shouted as she turned her face away with her arms up. She later looked at me.

"You weren't scared?" she asked.

I nodded. I was brave, emotionless. I had a cold personality.

After the fireworks were over, I went looking for Kunal.

"Where is Kunal? Can we wait for Kunal?" I asked the group I was with.

We all stood and waited. There were a lot of people around. So, I kept looking and finally found Kunal.

"Hey, Kunal!" I said.

He walked up to us with a smile with his hands in his pockets. He thought we had left him.

***

While the others decided to go somewhere else, I stayed with Kunal and the pretty girl who was from India on the metro train. Kunal was rubbing her leg, flirting with her. I couldn't really hear what they were saying, but I heard Kunal say.

"Why aren't you as sweet as Nabby?" he kept asking her.

Those two decided to go somewhere to eat, but I decided to stay on the metro train and go back to the dorm. I didn't want another Savannah and Jay situation, another Jeff and Marilynn situation, or another Byron and Mimosa situation. I came to Paris to have fun, not to deal with a man.

Kunal and the young Indian woman stepped off the train.

"Come with us?" Kunal asked me.

I shook my head. "I'm tired."

The subway doors slid closed and the subway went into the tunnel. The train suddenly stopped because someone pushed the emergency button. Then a few minutes later, it moved again.

At the metro station near the dorm, I met the copper-skin-toned, young Black woman who was an FSU student.

"You didn't want to go with Kunal and the Indian woman?" she asked.

I figured it must be a set up because men always want two women to fight over them.

"Oh, I let them be alone together," I said.

***

At the dorm, I went into her room and hung out with her and the other Black female FSU student, listening to the music on the radio. Kunal walked in. He sat next to me as the women were talking. I was mostly quiet and passive, plus I can't hear much. I asked Kunal if I could kiss his cheek.

"Sure," he said.

I kissed him.

"Ouch, that hurt my lips," I said.

"He needs to shave," one of the young black women said.

I couldn't believe that the hair on the face can be that sharp.

***

I went to the Delta Airline Paris City Office to tell them that my return ticket was stolen. They charged me fifty dollars for a replacement. It was the year 2000, I guess they didn't have those machine that scan plane tickets.

***

I saw Kunal shirtless, hair all over his chest. It was at night. Dark hallway. I walked upstairs and gave him a hug. We looked down. The blonde-haired overweight woman with a grimace, who messed up my film roll, was downstairs, spying on us. I didn't know what the deal was with her.

"Why can't I get a girlfriend?" he asked.

"We don't want you to have one, we want you to be a temporary boyfriend to all of us," I answered.

"Oh okay, I see," he said.

He looked down, feeling sorry for himself. I waved at him as I walked downstairs heading toward my dorm room.

"Bye Kunal," I said.

"Night," Kunal said.

***

Morning time, my bags and luggage were packed up. I left my dorm room and went downstairs. I signaled the receptionist in the dorm lobby to call a cab because she only spoke French. The receptionist was sitting at her four-foot-tall desk. She dialed the cab. I waited in the lobby by the door, with my luggage and bags near me.

***

The flight back to the United States was no problem. Except, two Black middle-aged women on the plane were blocking the restroom with an attitude.

"Say excuse me!" they said.

"Excuse me," I said softly.

They moved and I entered the restroom. Then after I was done, I exited the restroom, and they still frowned at me for no reason. I ignored them and sat back down.

***

I really enjoyed Paris. I guess that what I needed to do is be passive. So, I was passive during the Fall semester of 2000 at Gallaudet. Yes, I went back to Gallaudet.

Nabby

Amboise castle in France

MANGEORGE

(timeframe: 2000)

Dear Isa,

I re-enrolled at Gallaudet in 2000. No Jeff around. There were some new people. My African roommate was shorter than me, with chocolate-like skin. She spoke English clearly and even a bit of sign language. We stayed at Peet Hall, near the Kellogg Conference Hotel, and shared a bathroom with our floor.

***

I had new classmates. I was hoping that no men would mistreat me. I took film classes at Gallaudet with Professor Montenegro, a tall, average-looking, gay white man. He had us watching gay videos in class.

***

My roommate introduced me to her friend from Botswana. I didn't remember his full name, but he shortened it to Jeff. He was cute, shorter than me, light complexion, and had a big butt like mine. Once when I was trying to watch "*Xena*" on my roommate's TV, he suggested that I marry him and help him get his green card.

"Why didn't you ask someone else, maybe her other friend who was here a while ago?" I asked him.

My African roommate had another friend who was a young white woman with blonde hair who always wore shorts that showed off her shaky, fat legs.

"Eww, no, no, no," he signed.

I didn't get his attraction. A fat woman could always lose weight, but I couldn't fix my disfigured face and ears. I was nearly thirty years old, I could still get pregnant, and I didn't want to pass my birth defect on to my kids. But I didn't want to take birth control pills or anything.

***

The cafeteria was about five hundred feet from the dorm. It took forever to walk there from the Peet hall. I could have gone to the smaller cafeteria in the Student Academic Center, but I liked the bigger one because it had more food. So, I ran to the cafeteria every day for breakfast, lunch, and dinner.

It was at the larger cafeteria where I first met Wendy. She was a short-haired brunette who wore glasses, and she was using the walker because her bones couldn't handle her weight. I could always sit with her at the cafeteria, and we became good friends.

***

In the dorm room, African Jeff was still talking to me. I called him African Jeff because he wasn't the same

Jeff I met in 1996. The other Jeff had graduated and was gone, so now I had to deal with another Jeff.

"You can come with me to Botswana to meet my family," he said.

I didn't want to marry African Jeff and have to go to Botswana with him. I heard that in Africa, women had their genitals mutilated, and I didn't want them to do that to me. I didn't know if my roommate had gone through with it. She told me that she has human papillomavirus (HPV). I didn't know why she would tell me that. The dorm room was freezing because my roommate liked to leave the air conditioner on high. So, I went to the resident advisor and asked to move.

***

Eventually, I moved into what I thought was an empty room across from my old room, but someone else had already moved in. She didn't mind me cleaning up the place, rearranging the desks, and other stuff. She was Vietnamese and had short black hair. Her ex-boyfriend, George sometimes dropped by to visit. He was a five feet eight inches tall, ugly, bald white guy, but he fed us Chinese food. My roommate told me that she didn't like George because he was bald. I chatted with George a little bit, but I didn't remember the conversations.

***

Steve was a short, deaf, white guy with dark hair and black-rimmed glasses. He looked like Woody Allen with straight hair. He became my film partner, and we made a short film for our class with stuffed animal actors because we didn't want to ask anyone to act in our film.

He walked so fast and I tried to keep up with him, but I often stumbled in my ankle boots. He laughed so hard and apologized at the same time.

"Are you okay?" he asked.

"Yeah, could you please slow down?" I answered.

It didn't make sense to me why people were always rushing.

***

In my class, there was a deaf white guy who said he was from Ireland. He had such pretty, wide eyes. He told Professor Montenegro and our class how he became deaf.

"When I was a toddler," he signed. "I reached up with my hand and pulled down a pot of hot water. The hot water severely burned my back—third-degree burns. I was screaming so loud it caused my eardrums to burst. I had to have skin grafts from another part of my body to cover my back."

He showed a picture of his back to the class.

***

After we became close friends, Wendy asked me to move into her dorm. So, I moved from Peet Hall into Carlin Hall. This time, I only shared a bathroom with two people: Wendy and the religious woman with long brown-hair who worked part-time at the library. Wendy's dorm had three private rooms and that was so cool. I didn't need to walk far to the cafeteria because it was across from Carlin Hall.

After I moved there, we would go to the Union station together on the Gallaudet shuttle bus. Then a blonde-haired girl joined us. I forgot her name.

***

I was cracking jokes in the TFP department lobby and asked the tall, handsome Italian deaf guy.

"Are you a member of the Mafia?"

He made a "WTF" Italian hand gesture and then "Are you scared?" Italian hand gesture and the white male student who was watching us, laughed.

We waited for the class to start. Sometimes the professor had a class in the lobby; there were only six of us there, and the TV next to him showed us more gay movies.

***

As I walked back to my new dorm, the Irish guy with the burned back was in the lobby. As I was about to close the door of my dorm room after the long day from class, he waved at me.

"Need DirecTV," he signed.

"What? DirecTV?" I asked him.

I sat next to him, and then my tall, dark-skinned black neighbor sat down, too. We were watching a commercial, "*Girls Gone Wild*". Women were flashing their breasts on the overhead TV.

"Oh, that's nothing," he signed.

"You wanna see mine?" I joked.

My neighbor frowned at me. I grinned.

***

The next day, Steve and I were filming an object outside next to the Student Academic Center. An obese guy with a light brown complexion stood nearby. I waved at him and he waved back. I had seen him around Benson Hall a lot. I asked him how he made his hair so curly a few weeks ago before Steve and I were filming.

"I washed it and then put gel in it," he said.

But that was it. He stood there like he wanted something. I couldn't read his mind. When he only stood there, Steve and I went ahead and started filming. A few minutes later, I looked up and he had disappeared.

***

In my dorm room, I put a California State University of Northridge (CSUN) postcard on top of the chest. I was so curious about what it would be like if I went there. They had been the first university to offer integrated programs for deaf students, which had become the National Center on Deafness (NCOD).

***

A student was killed on Gallaudet's campus. The victim had severe cerebral palsy and was gay. I guess he thought the murderer was interested in him. The campus police found him in his dorm room in North Ballad Hall. It was scary to be at Gallaudet at the time, we didn't know who the murderer was. Some people thought I was, maybe because I'm Black and ugly. I took it as a sign that I should transfer to CSUN.

***

In the lobby of the TFP department, where the professor had makeshift classrooms, was a computer at the corner on the table. The bearded guy who copied off my ideas while peeking at my script a few years ago was still at Gallaudet. He was checking the presidential election result on the Internet.

"Bush is winning," I told him.

He responded in sign language. "No, no, no!"

I grinned. "Ha-ha, Bush is gonna be our President!"

Yeah, I'm a Black Republican.

Dylan wasn't there. Even that Ed Morrow-wannabe professor wasn't there. Things changed then because I heard that the TFP department was having problems... things were out of control right after I left Gallaudet in 1997.

There was a surgical scar on Dean Jane Norman's chest as if she had a heart implant or something. She was sitting at her desk. I just waved hi to her. She didn't teach any of the classes I took.

Professor Montenegro had come from Argentina. I had never seen a white Hispanic guy before. I thought all Hispanic people were brown. I heard him talking to someone on the phone in Spanish in his office.

***

I was riding the Gallaudet shuttle bus to Union Station to get a break from the dorm. I saw Poorna on the shuttle bus.

"Hi, how are you?" I signed to her.

"I'm fine. This is my husband. He's from India," she signed.

Her husband was handsome and taller than she was. She was lucky she didn't have my problem: my facial deformity and how people treated me. Her life seemed so normal. Probably an arranged marriage or not. I googled her and I saw a picture of her, her husband, and two sons. She had her doctorate in psychology and was working as a professor at Gallaudet.

I did see Alex, again. He and his former blonde hair girlfriend were still at Gallaudet. I wondered what his former girlfriend thought about seeing me again, after Jeff's and my fight in her dorm room in 1997. I didn't see Diedre and Chris; I think they were ashamed of me after my fight with Jeff.

***

Steve and I were making another film project; we filmed the Lincoln Memorial. I didn't remember how we got there since we didn't have a car. I guessed we took the shuttle bus and then rode the train from Union Station to the National Mall. We also filmed the Jefferson Memorial. We were sightseeing while we filmed. After we finished filming, we had to climb a grassy hill to get on the sidewalk. As we went up, I was behind him, and he took my hand to help me up. I felt he was a romantic gentleman, but after what Bobby and Jeff did to me, I was protecting my heart. I wasn't asking anyone for sex, either. We must have taken the bus because I remember waiting for a while on Fourteenth Street.

***

In the dorm, I was with Wendy and our blonde-haired friend whose name I couldn't remember, and we had recently gotten back from the Union Station. Wendy had gotten a new mobility scooter with the help of Medicaid. Our blonde friend saw the cute young man from Ireland in the lobby and I saw her walk shyly away.

"She likes you," I told the Irish fellow.

I smiled. He stared at me but didn't say anything, as if he was trying to say that he liked me. The burns on his back shouldn't compare to my deformed face. With his cute face and wide, brown eyes, any woman could be with him; they wouldn't care about his back. He could cover it up with a shirt. I understood he had some insecurities, though. But people would want to know why I was with him, and I wouldn't feel like explaining.

I didn't know anything about white guys. I never dated men, so I didn't know anything about dating or having a boyfriend, either. Maybe his family in Ireland wouldn't accept me. I didn't know how people in Ireland were and I didn't want to suffer heartache to find out.

***

It seemed like I was having a great time without a man in my life. I didn't go back to Gallaudet for the spring semester in 2001. It was good that Jeff wasn't there. I was happy that I had met Wendy and other people, but I decided to go to CSUN. I was hoping to meet the same type of people and to have a nice time at CSUN.

***

The murder on the Gallaudet campus freaked me out, but they finally caught the killer during the spring semester in 2001 after he killed another male student. When it happened, I was at home with my mom on Don Street in Memphis, applying to CSUN.

***

I didn't write much about George. George must be an Angel. I never did know if he was interested in me, romantically or sexually, or wanted to be my friend. I saw George at the California State University of Northridge. If you read the *"Erwicked" chapter*, you'll see what I mean when I said George was an angel.

Nabby

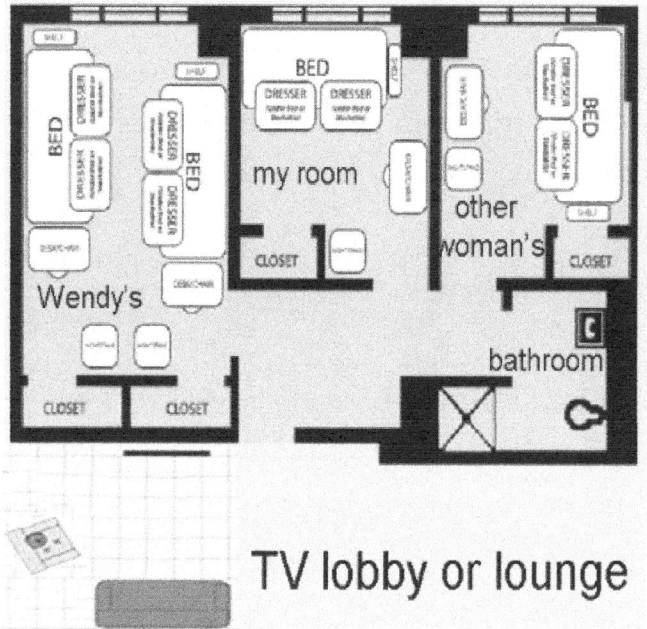

Gallaudet tv studio

ERWICKED

(timeframe: 2001 – 2003)

Dear Isa,

During the summer of 2001, I was chatting with deaf people in AOL chat rooms and while I was on the computer, I was reading the CSUN catalog. That was why I didn't judge actress Lori Loughlin and others who got in trouble trying to get their kids into big schools. It was hard to get into CSUN. After reading the CSUN catalog, I had to have an excellent GPA, excellent ACT score, and so on.

I filled out the International (Foreign) Student Admission application online. All I needed to do was put down my name, date of birth, and a fake birthplace. That was it. That was how simple it was. Then a few weeks later, I got a letter stating that I was accepted at CSUN.

I was like wow.

"That was so simple," I said to myself.

I even got a dorm room. At least I didn't have to pay half of million dollars to get into one of the California colleges.

CSUN was in Northridge, California, forty-six miles from Los Angeles. I didn't get to see Los Angeles or Hollywood much while I was there. CSUN was at 18111 Nordhoff Street.

***

During this time, I used a walker because so I could have the whole bedroom all myself with no roommate. I told Housing that I had multiple sclerosis (MS). I learned that from Wendy. I was staying in building fifteen, Bougainvillea Hall. There was no kitchen, just two bedrooms, a bathroom, and the living room. I only had a Hispanic roommate and an Asian roommate. My two roommates had to sleep in the other bedroom. I forgot what floor I was on.

***

I did a new student orientation with the deaf students at the National Center on Deafness (NCOD), which was in Jeanne M. Chisholm Hall. I was curious about who the deaf students were. That was how I met Eric in person. I saw his picture with a group of deaf students and NCOD staff online. I wanted to meet him.

On the first day of new student orientation, I saw Eric, a tall, athletic, okay-looking, Hispanic deaf guy. He was the leader of the group, leading new students to places such as camping in cabins in the woods, and trips to Universal Studios and the beach.

We had orientation in the lounge at NCOD. It had a few sofas, TV, and things for deaf people to hang out. Sometimes they served pizza and other types of food there. There were also a few offices for deaf fraternity and sorority. I was cracking jokes with Eric, while we were waiting for other new deaf students to join.

The next day, I decided not to do the rest of the orientation. My memories of Bobby, Jeff, and Pierre really traumatized me. Staying at the dorm, I thought, might help me avoid problems with men.

***

During the spring of 2001, I changed my classes from the Intensive English Program to Master of Arts Degree in Special Education program. I took American Sign Language class, Deaf Studies, and Introduction to Disability Studies so I could become a special education teacher. I was getting a master's degree. I already knew American Sign Language, that's why it was the easiest class.

In Deaf Studies class, I felt so laid back. No Jeff, no Bobby, a new life, start fresh. Then Eric walked in. I pretended I didn't see him. Why couldn't I go to college without a man on my side? There would always be a problem. I didn't have a problem with Kunal, but if Eric wanted to use me to get a girlfriend, then I wouldn't help him. If men have problems finding a girlfriend, then they should punish the women they really wanted, not me.

I also didn't want him to find out I have a criminal record. I didn't want to tell everyone I have a criminal record and have them judge me. Plus, I didn't have any money to give him if he is like Bobby.

After the class was over, I picked up my book, got up from my desk, stepped down from five steps, walked toward the rear door of the classroom. Eric's eyes met mine, but I didn't speak to him. I just walked out the door.

***

As I walked near the southeast of campus, I saw a few production recreational vehicles (RV). A pretty, young black woman was stepping out of one of the production RVs. I thought that was cool. Maybe one day I'll have millions of dollars to produce a film, to rent some of these production RVs and hire some actors. Most people didn't understand me, they thought I should be like them: get married, have kids, and get a regular job.

***

During the Introduction to Disability Studies class, I knew I shouldn't be in that class. I knew that I couldn't be a special ed teacher. People working for the government must have a clean background check. Plus, I wasn't interested in teaching.

***

I dropped out of the Master of Arts Degree in Special Education program a few days later, but still attended Deaf Studies and ASL class. The professor of that program approached me. She was in her late forties, a white woman with eyeglasses with brownish short hair. I forgot what the conversation was about. But I think she wanted to encourage me to be a special ed teacher. Well, because of the way I look, I didn't think children would want to be around me.

***

I tried not to go to NCOD as much, knowing that Eric might be around there. There were a lot of activities and events for deaf students to go to.

I went to my dorm room and I couldn't get into the room. The key was fine and the doorknob was fine. I saw a shadow at the bottom of the door as if someone was blocking it. I pushed the door so hard that my tall, overweight Hispanic roommate finally stopped barricading the door with her body. I never had a conversation with her. I didn't even know her name. I just walked straight to my bedroom. I spent most of the time in the bedroom anyway, I didn't know why she blocked the door. She could always move out and find another dorm room.

I bought a toy bug and pinned it on top of my hat. I went to deaf studies class, hoping that Eric didn't want me at all. During class, all I felt was him staring at me until the class was over.

***

I stopped using the walker. I asked the CSUN Student Housing Office if I could move into the Deaf dorm, building six aka Pacific Willow Hall because my roommate barricading the door to keep me out disturbed me. Plus, the cafeteria and the mailboxes were closer to Pacific Willow Hall. They approved and allowed me to move there. So, I moved all my things into the Deaf dorm. The Deaf dorm has many deaf students living there. I knew Eric lived off-campus, so I wouldn't run into him at the Deaf dorm. There were no deaf black men and a few deaf black women.

***

NCOD had many events and activities. I tried to avoid a lot of those because Eric might be there. One day I went to get some pizza at the deaf lounge. I saw Eric at the NCOD, standing at the outside living space of Jeanne Chisholm Hall with his male friends, near the deaf lounge's door. I didn't want to be rude, so I spoke to them.

"Too late, too late!" Eric signed.

He walked inside the deaf lounge.

I followed him and saw him enter one of the small offices. He sat in a chair while a white deaf woman with long, blonde hair sat at the desk opposite him. That must be his ex-girlfriend, because of the way he ran to her. I felt I would be in another triangle relationship, like Jay and Savannah, Byron and Mimosa, and Jeff and Marilynn. So, I left the NCOD lounge. I later learned that it was his ex-girlfriend, someone confirmed it.

***

I rode the CSUN shuttle bus a lot because my classes were farthest away from the Deaf dorm. I walked from Pacific Willow Hall and had to cross Lassen Street at the light to get to the F10 parking lot. I got on the shuttle bus, and it had to wait for about fifteen to thirty minutes. Then it drove off the parking lot, turned left onto Lindley Avenue, then turned right onto Lassen Street, right on Reseda Boulevard, and then right onto the CSUN campus. It parked near the curb and that was where I stepped down from the bus and walked to my morning class.

***

On Saturday, my pretty blonde-haired white deaf roommate brought in her deaf friends. One of them was Eric's closest fraternity friend. They sat in our dorm's living room on the couch and invited me to sit with them.

"Eric moved on, so sorry," My roommate signed.

"Well, he can kiss my ass," I signed.

We laughed, but Eric's best friend didn't. I knew he was going to tell Eric. I wished I hadn't said that. I wished I said I wasn't interested in Eric. I just made things worse. I didn't know that Eric would turn out to be like Jeff.

***

My blonde-haired roommate moved out. My brunette-haired roommate, Heather, moved out of the bedroom I was in and moved into my Asian roommate's bedroom. Heather and the Asian roommate were not deaf.

It was cool to have a room all by myself. I put my TV near the window on top of the nightstand and I changed to another bed, which was in a better position. I also closed my door and locked it. I had my privacy.

***

2001 was the year Aaliyah died. I grieved for her and couldn't believe she was gone. She was one of my favorite singers.

***

Later that year, I woke up and looked on TV, two buildings were on fire in New York City. They said the plane had crashed into them. I couldn't think. Maybe it was a terrible accident. I dressed up and left the room to go to class.

In the ASL class, my brown-haired white professor turned on the TV overhead because she was concerned about her friends and family members in NYC. The classmates and I were watching the LIVE news about the 9/11 tragedy.

"I need to cancel this class today. You guys can go," she signed to us.

So, I left there and walked back to my dorm room. I turned on my TV and as I stood in front of it, I saw the two buildings falling. I was shocked.

***

In the spring semester of 2002, my bike was stolen. I usually parked my bike near building three, aka Woodruff Hall. Maybe people were concerned about me riding the bike or if it was part of Eric's revenge for saying he can kiss my ass.

***

I saw so many beautiful female students on campus. I didn't get why Eric didn't go after one of them. Why would he want me, a woman with deformed ears and face? Why couldn't men just move on? If I don't want them, they can go search for someone else who wants to love them. I didn't bother to contact the police or anything. I bought another bike and parked it in my bedroom.

***

I didn't see Eric anymore. He wasn't in any of my classes. In American Deaf Culture class, Heather was in that class. She sat nearly at the back. I sat in the front row. Near the end of the class, an overweight, deaf white woman was passing out flyers for the deaf event at the NCOD. She looked like a lesbian with a boyish look. Before she gave a flyer to me, she scorned at me, pointing her index finger in my face. I didn't understand what she said. The tall, fifty years old professor shook his head and Heather quickly left the class. I felt Eric's wrath, again.

***

During the summer, I didn't take any classes. I had to move into the building seven, Torrey Pine Hall. Both building seven and six had a kitchen. I lived alone with no roommates. Nobody can bother me. Everything seemed so peaceful. That was why I love to live alone. I was mostly introverted. I didn't like to socialize. So, I didn't know why people think I should have friends or a boyfriend/husband. I didn't talk to anyone that much. I just liked being on the internet and spent almost fifteen hours a day on it.

***

I went out only to buy groceries. A few times I got locked out of the building. I didn't understand why they would lock the front door in the summer.

I locked myself out of the building again with a bag of groceries in my bike basket, with nobody around to open the door. I waited for nearly an hour. My milk and meat were going bad. The sun was blazing down on me. It was summer in California, about a hundred degrees.

There was a fire alarm outside of the building. So, I pulled it down. I didn't expect the firemen with their fire trucks to come over. I just thought dorm residents would exit and stand outside. After a dorm resident opened the door to get out of the building, I held the door before it swung shut and entered the building.

I didn't understand why CSUN won't let us use the key card to scan in the keycard reader.

How will the dorm residents be able to go to summer class every day and be able to go back in? I didn't know if Eric was doing this or that was CSUN rules. If Eric was doing this, then he was so evil. If CSUN was doing it, then they were racist. I guess they didn't want a black woman to do well in college.

I did believe that Eric had that much power because he was a popular swimming athlete at CSUN.

Celebrities have power. Their fan would do anything for them. For example, V. Stiviano got punched in the mouth by LA Lakers owner Donald Sterling's fan for telling everyone that he was a racist.

***

In the fall semester of 2002, I had two new roommates. They were both Black. I thought I wouldn't have a problem with them, but they were worse than the Black roommates in the Atlanta Job Corps dorm.
I took a scriptwriting class, which was my favorite class ever. I did a new student orientation again at NCOD and met new deaf students. The leader of the new student orientation was Eric's best friend. The one who saw me sign, "Eric can kiss my ass." I meant it as a joke. Eric's best friend was an average-looking young white male, with a hearing problem.

During orientation, the new deaf students and I rode in cars to go to Universal Citywalk. There were fifteen of us. Our group was broken up into small groups of three or four. So, I ended up with Patty and the other girl. Patty spent sixty minutes in one store because she looked at almost a dozen shirts on a rack for five minutes per shirt. I was not a shopper. I didn't look at clothing materials and designs. I would just pick something pretty, then buy it. There was nothing I was interested in buying at the Universal Citywalk.

Finally, we were out of that store. Patty didn't want to go to another store, she wanted to go to sit at the Hard Rock Cafe, where the leaders said they would be. Everybody had to go to the HRC at a certain time so they could count how many people were there so that they don't leave anyone behind or start looking for a missing person, but it was too early to meet with the leaders.

Another group invited me. One of them was from North Korea with a burned arm and missing fingers.

"Let's go," he told us.

We would enter one store and stay in there for a minute, then we would run out and would hop into another store, and then repeat the cycle. He was so fun to be with. I hoped that we wouldn't get into trouble for being wild.

The Korean led us to the Hard Rock Cafe because time was up. When we arrived, the leaders said we could order something to eat. They were paying the bill. I sat with the Korean guy and others. I ordered crispy chicken nuggets. While we waited for our order, he looked at me.

"What happened to your face?" he signed.

"I was born that way," I signed back.

I already knew what happened to his arm. There was a war in North Korea when he was a toddler. The military burned down his house and he was hurt. An American couple adopted him. He told his story at the NCOD on the first day of Orientation when we were introducing each other.

Our meals arrived. I really enjoyed being with him. I thought we had something in common. My face messed up and his arm messed up. But I was thirty-one and he was twenty. Eric was about his age.

Yeah, I was thirty-one years old, still at college. I felt like high school was a waste of time. Everybody should go to college at age fifteen, instead of eighteen. Then we would have time to know what we really want to do or be, instead of reading about Shakespeare, algebra, learning about health, and physical education—most of us will become overweight anyway. Also, all of us won't work as engineers. Instead of learning about "*Romeo and Juliet*", we should be learning about how to run a business, how to get some loans, farm experience, and trade skills.

After we ate at Hard Rock Cafe, the leaders decided it was time to go back to CSUN. I hugged the Korean guy. Eric's best friend looked down and shook his head.

The next day was our trip to the beach. Eric's best friend wanted me to ride with him in his "cool" vehicle. He blasted nothing but his rap music. We traveled far from CSUN to the beach. We finally arrived at the beach and I didn't see the Korean guy. We waited for the Korean guy and others, but they didn't show up. So, the leaders broke us up and put us in groups again.

"You with her," the leader said.

So, I was with Patty. The boring Patty. They probably knew I wanted to hang out with the Korean guy. Someone who understood what it was like to be different. I couldn't be with someone who was different. I had to be with people who were ignorant and wanted to talk down to me.

I went to the clothing store with Patty again and was bored to death because she only looked at clothes for a long time like she had the previous day.

Patty kept telling me to look. "How you like it?" I didn't say anything. I was not a shopper. I went to the tattoo vendor for a temporary tattoo. Something I can press on my body with water. I was thinking about covering my old scar with it. Patty wasn't interested, she tried to persuade me to look at clothes. She gave up on me and we sat at the table for two hours. We didn't walk along the beach sidewalk or anything. I paid two hundred dollars for this orientation. I didn't pay just to shop at one store and to sit at the table until the leaders came back with the groups. I hope Patty didn't expect me to be her friend after that.

The next day, we were supposed to go camping. I didn't go, because I felt that the leaders will partner me with Patty again. I just stayed in my dorm room.

I saw what I thought was Bobby's car, an old light tan 60s classic car. It was parked at a gas station nearby CSUN on Reseda. I thought it may have been my imagination. Maybe, Bobby, I met at FSU, was haunting me.

I really liked my face before I had reconstruction surgery. Boys didn't like my face back then. I wished I didn't have surgery to look a little better. My earlier life was so much better. Being called a monkey by black kids wasn't so bad at all. If I didn't have surgery on my face, then men wouldn't bother me at all. My first goal was to experience sex and a man was needed for that, now I have given up on men. I felt like most men were so obnoxious.

***

I finished up my short film script and needed to print it. I didn't have a printer in my dorm room. So, I emailed the script to myself and went downstairs to the computer lab. As I went inside the computer lab, a curly-haired, cute, short, deaf Hispanic-looking guy asked me.

"Did you go camping with the deaf orientation group?"

"No," I signed.

"You didn't go, because I didn't show up," he laughed.

I didn't say anything. It wasn't true at all. I wouldn't waste my time on a guy with a big ego. He probably thought I was in the computer lab because of him, too. I thought he was gay, because of his feminine traits.

I printed out my script and made a few copies for my classmates to read and give their critique.

***

George entered the computer lab. Yes, George who dated my former Asian roommate at Gallaudet.

"Television, Film and Photography department at Gallaudet is now closed," George signed.

Did he travel from Washington D.C. to California just to tell me that? We chatted a bit and then walked to his dorm room in building one, Chanterelle Hall. He had no kitchen and no living room. He must not know about the building six, Pacific Willow Hall, where the deaf residents stayed. He showed me his bedroom. I hoped he wasn't at CSUN to cause problems for me.

***

I sometimes rode on the CSUN shuttle bus. Many times, the bus left the parking lot right when I was closer to it. This time I was just ten feet away. I didn't want to wait for another bus, so I walked back to my dorm and squeezed the bike out of the two feet by four feet with seven feet height balcony closet because my roommates didn't want me to park my bike in the living room, even after I told them that my other bike was stolen. They were just being mean and evil. They had guests over every night in the living room. Sometimes parties. And I had never seen them studying. There was no elevator, but it was cool as I only stayed on the second floor. I dragged the bike downstairs and rode to class.

***

My interpreter didn't show up in one of my classes, so I went to NCOD to request an interpreter.

"You need to go see a psychologist!" my NCOD advisor said with an attitude.

I didn't know why I needed to seek help. If there was a shortage of interpreters, I felt she should have told me.

So, I did what she wanted me to do and went to University Counseling Services. The psychologist was a black man. I had an ASL interpreter there.

"Did you watch "*227*" TV show?" he asked.

"Yes," I responded.

"The man that plays Lester Jenkins is my friend."

I didn't understand what that had to do with me.

"You think you will become a successful filmmaker because of your disability," he continued to say.

That was not what I was thinking at all.

"You are using your disability as a crutch," he continued to say.

What about that man, paralyzed from the neck down, in my scriptwriting class? Nobody criticized him. He couldn't use his leg and arms. He couldn't talk at all. He sat in the electric wheelchair parked in front of the class. And people criticized me for taking a film class. I didn't get it. All I had was a hearing problem. I can walk and do most things, but he couldn't. I guess it had something to do with my gender, I was a female and he was a male. Maybe it was something to do with my race since I was Black and he was white. We were about the same age. I felt like seeing a psychologist was a waste of my fucking time. Men just wanted me to become a housewife. This was 2002, not the 1950s. I didn't like how men think. I forgot I was the only black person in those film classes. I never really thought about it at all. They were racist and ignorant then. I felt everyone should learn anything they wish to learn. It should be our rights.

***

I rode one of the shuttle buses and saw George. I sat next to him and we chatted. I forgot where I was going or why I had to ride the shuttle bus. George asked me if I could go to the museum with him one day.

"That's fine," I said.

"Let stay in touch," George said.

We exchanged email addresses.

***

Later, housing evicted me from the dorm because of my issues with my roommates. I stayed at the hotel nearby and asked my mom to send some money so I could stay until I finished classes. I rode my bike from the hotel to my CSUN classes. I didn't give up. Nothing would tear me down. The hotel was the ugliest hotel I have ever been in, but it was cheap. I saw some other people living in the hotel. I didn't know you could live in a hotel. Cigarette burns marks were on the wall and an unknown substance stained the towels brown.

***

Fall semester was almost over. I went to the CSUN's library and re-enrolled at Gallaudet for the spring of 2003. Then after the semester was over, I gave my bike to Goodwill. I packed my things up and flew to Washington D.C.

I took beginner photography and a film class. I couldn't find Wendy at Carlin Hall. I was in the same dorm room where Wendy, a religious woman, and I were living in on the first floor. I didn't know how things can change that much in two years. Maybe the murders were scaring everyone away.

"Where are you?" George emailed me from California.

"At Gallaudet," I emailed him back.

That was the last time I contacted George.

I was glad that he told me the T.F.P. dept was closing. George was right, so much was changing. I guessed Gallaudet was trying to save money. Hollywood and television news studios wouldn't hire a deaf person anyway. I wouldn't ever forget George buying Chinese food for my Asian roommate and me in 2000. I wouldn't forget when my roommate told me he didn't give her good oral sex. It was kinda gross that he ate pussy, his face and mouth were on a vagina.

Gallaudet did shut down the Television, Film, and Photography department, but they still had T.F.P classes at the Washburn Arts Building (WAB), next to the Kellogg Conference Hotel. I simply walked from Carlin Hall, across Hanson Plaza, and then finally to the WAB. A nice walk I took every weekday.

***

In the film class at the WAB, my white female blonde-haired professor didn't think I was able to learn film because of my appearance and maybe because I was the only black student. She wanted a white dark-haired deaf guy and me to come with her to her office. We arrived at her small office, which was twice the size of the closet. She showed a video game and told me the guy with us made it. At first, I was shocked. I thought I had to be as good as he was, and I didn't deserve to be in the T.F.P. I asked his name and he told me.

"How come your name isn't on the credit list?" I asked him.

My professor was dumbfounded. So, she asked him to make an abstract short film so he could prove her point.

"Okay, I will," he signed.

I had to do an abstract short film, too.

Her point being that I couldn't be part of the course because of my appearance. Sadly, many people would've agree with her.

***

I went on the DC duck tour and took photos of the sightseeing and the boat for my photography class. I used the 1960s Nikon camera that only produced black and white photos. After that, I had to go to the darkroom to develop the pictures. During photography class, I showed my pictures through the projector.

"It's good," said one of my classmates.

"Blurry, all of your pictures are blurry," Professor Grandstaf signed.

I guess I shook the camera too much while taking pictures. Dr. Grandstaf never taught us how to take pictures. He should have taken the class outside and taught us how to take pictures. He needed to teach us how to operate the camera, manually. This was 2003, and Gallaudet didn't give us updated cameras like Canon and Nokia digital cameras, even for beginning photography students.

***

At the film class, I showed my abstract short film.

"You did a good job, it looks like something is behind the box," the professor said.

Then it was the white brunette deaf man's turn. He showed us a video of him filming through the airplane window of its landing. The professor was so embarrassed. She realized I had more film skills than him. She thought I would have less skill than him. That was sad because she was a female just like me. She should have known better. Women need to stick together, not support some white males.

***

In photography class, the other students went to Sweden, leaving just me and another female student in the classroom. I didn't remember if Dr. Grandstaf went. I didn't want to be bothered with that African American doctor at the campus medical clinic and have him say I couldn't go because I was anemic.

***

At my dorm, I emailed many Gallaudet staff how I felt about them closing the T.F.P. department. I typed that I would kill myself, but that was just something I said. I had no intention of harming myself. Unfortunately, Dr. Grandstaf took it personally.

He invited me to his office at the WAB and suggested I seek counseling. He said he could help me graduate from Gallaudet.

"Fine, I will go seek counseling," I signed.

I thought he was bargaining with me. Dr. Grandstaf had short shaved peppered hair with a goatee, about forty-five years old. He's married and had kids.

***

At the cafeteria, I ate at the table alone as usual. African Jeff was sitting with a white woman next to him at another table. He waved at me. I waved back, but I didn't want to talk to him, because he may say, "This woman married me and helped me get a green card. Too bad you didn't help me." You know how some people are. They would have some sort of attitude. I quickly ate my meal and rushed back to my dorm.

***

I received a letter from the administrative office, stating that I needed to finish up minor classes such as English, Math, and so on. I went to see Dr. Grandstaf at his office and he suggested that I take Beginner Photography again, even though I received a C in that class Still, he wanted me to take it again. I didn't know why he hates me so much. I walked back to my dorm, trying to think.

***

In my dorm room, I read the Gallaudet catalog book, "Students who have previously earned B.A., B.S. or higher degrees from colleges/universities other than

Gallaudet must satisfy only the second B.A. or B.S. degree's major prerequisites and requirements. Students must also earn thirty credits or more in order to graduate with a second degree."

I had received my college degree from LeMoyne Owen College in 1999, and I took more than thirty credits of classes at Gallaudet. I rushed to the Office of Administrative at the College Hall and told the staff there I already got a college degree. I had to point out the rule to them in the catalog.

"You need to get the transcript from LeMoyne Owen College and also a statement that you graduated from there," one of the staff signed.

"Okay," I signed.

***

On my way to my film class, walking through Hanson Plaza, there were familiar faces. The young men looked so familiar. I looked back, thinking, "Are these guys from CSUN?" I wondered if I was imagining things.

***

At the film class, my professor was a blond average looking, white woman. She wasn't deaf. She just seemed like she wanted to help deaf people. Dr. Grandstaf was tone-deaf and couldn't talk. The blonde professor, I forgot her name, could hear and could talk well.

"Gallaudet is closing T.F.P. for good and if you want to continue to learn film, then I suggest that you go to New York Film Academy. But it is hard to get into because many applicants want to go there," she signed.

I went to New York Film Academy (NYFA) in 2007 in Los Angeles. If she hadn't mentioned it, I would have never heard about this school. It was an okay experience at NYFA, but I didn't really like it.

***

I received a sealed envelope from LeMoyne Owen College. It didn't take long for LOC to mail it to me after I ordered the transcript and degree verification letter. I couldn't open it. So, I walked from the Student Academic Center to the College Hall and gave the staff at the office of Administration, the envelope. The two staff opened the envelope and read the letter. They seemed to be in shock. I didn't remember afterward, but I was ecstatic.

I entered the Student Academic Center building with a smile. I saw Eric sitting at the window seat in the hallway. He looked directly at me. I approached him.

"I will graduate," I told him.

"Lie," he responded in sign language.

He didn't even know me at all. That was why I don't like gossipers. He thought he knew me by listening to rumors. I sat next to him. Eric said he was here at Gallaudet to see his friends. I was like, "Okay, whatever."

A pretty, biracial young woman with long curly hair stood in front of us, talking to him and other students.

"Why not date her? She's pretty," I signed.

"She's a friend," he signed back.

I didn't understand. Why can't we just be friends? Instead of being angry and being vengeful toward me just because I wasn't interested in him. I got a fucked-up face and this girl was so beautiful. Why not go after her?

That was the last time I saw Eric. I left the SAC, went on to my dorm room, and locked my door. It was spring break week. I hid from him. I ate whatever I had in the mini-refrigerator and warmed it up in the microwave. I didn't want to go to the cafeteria, because I feared he would be there.

***

After spring break was over, I went to Dr. Grandstaf's office which was three times bigger than the blonde-haired professor's office.

"Why didn't you tell me that you had already gotten a degree from the previous college," Dr. Grandstaf said.

In my mind, I thought, "Fuck yeah, you better give me that damn college degree you promised me."

Instead, I responded to him. "I'm sorry."

***

I was staying at the Gallaudet dorm during the summer because I was planning to visit the Treacher Collins Syndrome yahoo group's party in Baltimore, Maryland to meet with other people who have a facial deformity. But my White roommate was giving me a hard time, so I went back home.

Nabby

CSUN Student Housing Map

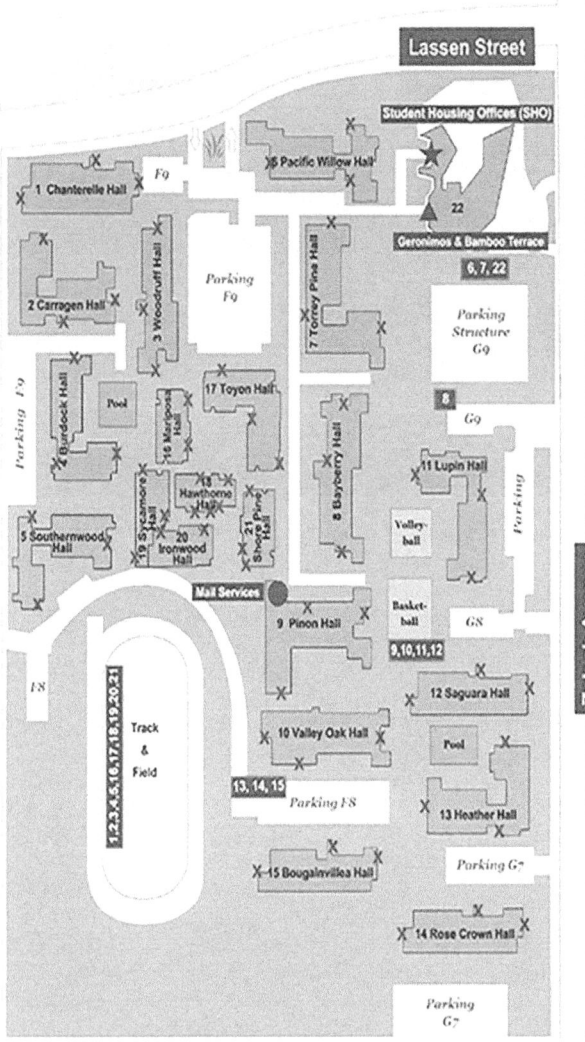

ROB BIRD

(timeframe: 2011 – 2013)

Dear Isa,

After I came back home, I emailed Dr. Grandstaf
and then I threatened him that I will use the email he
messaged me that he will give me my college degree to
sue if he won't give me my college degree. I didn't go to
graduation at Gallaudet because it was so sad how
Gallaudet treated me.

After I had gotten my second Bachelor of Arts
degree from Gallaudet, Gallaudet banned me from
coming to their campus. I guessed it was their plan; to
never give me my college degree. I was glad that I
threatened Dr. Grandstaf. Anyway, I put my second
bachelor's degree in a picture frame and hung it on my
wall.

***

From 2003 to 2007, I stayed at home. I was
staying at a new house because my mom moved from
Memphis to Northern Mississippi. I spent the years from
when I was thirty-two to thirty-six just being on the
internet at home. I didn't socialize or date anyone. I
wasn't like most women, who need to get married and
have children before they turn forty.

In Memphis or Northern Mississippi, there wasn't
much to do anyway. I didn't create a film or do anything

with my college degrees. I just stayed at home, on the Internet most of the time. Sometimes I went on a cruise with my mom and nephew. I went to Hawaii in 2003 and Alaska in 2005.

***

I went to the Northern Mississippi Vocational Rehabilitation's warehouse in 2007, with me working there. I wish to meet someone that looked like Usher, but I wish I was prettier though. I was playing Usher's CD in my car on my way to and from the Mississippi warehouse every weekday.

While working at Northern Mississippi Vocational Rehab's warehouse, a dark-skinned, short, black guy gave me a note. In the note, I read, "I like you." I threw that note away. The next day, he came up to me to confront me.

"I'm ugly," I told him.

"You're not ugly! My girlfriend is fat," he said.

Like that supposed to make me feel better. There was a quote, "I may be fat, but you're ugly, and I can lose weight." See there, men want me to compete. He got a girlfriend. What did I tell ya?

I was thirty-six years old, and I didn't want to get pregnant, passing on my gene to a child. I'm not using birth control pills, which may cause cancer. I didn't feel like explaining that to him. He might have said it wouldn't matter what the children looked like, but he wouldn't understand how life would treat them. I didn't want my children to be bullied because they have small, deformed ears or hound dog-looking eyes. He wouldn't have enough money to pay for them to get reconstruction surgery on their face.

I thought no meant no, I'm not interested. See, that is why sexual harassment at workplace exists. I shouldn't have to explain myself. But I guess I did have to because he took it personally.

He gave me his phone number. So, I called him after I came home because I was curious.

"Hello," he answered.

"It's me," I said.

"Golly, you call me! I can't believe it. Wait, my cell phone's battery is low, can you call back at four?" he hung up on me.

I didn't call him back, I thought maybe he was lying and wanted to play mind games. I threw his phone number away. I guess his girlfriend saw my phone number through caller ID on his cell phone. She probably asked him about me.

A few days later, his jealous girlfriend sat next to me at World Overcomers Church, and she kept swiping a pencil around my face, but she didn't have the courage to stab me. I knew that was his girlfriend because he asked me what church I went to. So, I decided to not go to that church anymore.

It didn't make sense, why do men want me to compete for them with another girl? This girl would have plucked out my eyeball. I didn't want to be a housewife. I didn't want him. I didn't want marriage. She would have plucked out my eyeball for nothing. My face was already fucked up, because I have a birth defect, deformity, and this woman wanted to pluck out my eye over some man that I didn't want at all. And what would he want a one-eyed wife for? To me he wasn't worth it, he was a short, brown-skinned Black man, and he looked like Usher.

He had a used car, I panicked because I thought he would follow me home when I was driving the red 2007 Ford Focus. I looked in the rear mirror every five minutes to make sure he wasn't following me. I didn't want someone toxic to come around my mom's house. He was working at a warehouse with me, making thirteen dollars a day, so his girlfriend could have him. I didn't want his ugly-ass kids. Congratulations to her, I hope she is happy with her award as a housewife: cleaning, cooking, and mingling with the in-laws. I didn't want a future with him.

***

I didn't look for another job, because I knew I would end up working at a warehouse or at Walmart. Wherever I worked, men would harass me and make my life so much worse because it was bad enough to live with Treacher Collins Syndrome and have people treat me differently.

I didn't understand why men think that my life would be so much better being with them. I had that experience with Kunal, Bobby, Jay, and Jeff and look at how those turned out. So why do I want to waste any more time with men and why did I need to bring children into this world? Most people will work as a nurse, Walmart cashier, police officer, or be homeless. I just didn't see any point in getting married and having children.

***

In the spring of 2008, I went back to CSUN because I was planning to search for an apartment while I attended. I was evicted from CSUN housing in 2002, but they allowed me back at the dorm. I was staying in building fifteen again, in the same dorm room I had where my Hispanic roommate blocked the door. But my old Hispanic roommate wasn't there, I had two new Hispanic roommates.

I was searching for the apartment and was surprised that I found one on 2619 Wilshire Boulevard in Los Angeles. I moved in April of 2008 into a studio apartment on the fifth floor. I was so happy to live independently, but the apartment was old and nasty. The rent was five hundred fifty dollars a month including the utility bill. I bought some furniture from a local furniture store. All I needed was a table with four chairs and a twin-sized bed. I didn't need a sofa because I didn't have people coming over anyway. I bought two cheap plastic nightstands, two metal bookshelves, four storage boxes, and two TV trays. I still had my small, gray Magnavox television, which I set on one of the TV trays. I placed my laptop on the other TV tray, and I would sit in front of the laptop while sitting in one of the chairs I bought with the table.

***

In 2011, I decided to go to vocational rehabilitation, which was at 3333 Wilshire Boulevard in Los Angeles. There I met Robert, who had long blonde hair, which was about fourteen inches. He was a tall, deaf white guy with blue eyes, who worked there as a counselor. He set me up with Renata. She was about forty years old, the same age I was. She had short, curly brown hair, an average body shape, and was about my height.

The next day, I met her in a conference meeting room. We sat at the table and she gave me an IQ test to see how smart I was. I felt so offended by that. However, I just told her that I had two college degrees. Just because I have a disability, that doesn't mean I am dumb.

"I had a guy here and he didn't pass the test. But you're smart," she said.

As if I didn't know. I know myself better than anyone else does. I didn't need someone to tell me that I am smart. That was a big waste of time.

On another day, Renata and I went to a building where the Screen Actors Guild (SAG) and the American Federation of Television and Radio Artists (AFTRA) was on 5757 Wilshire Boulevard. They were having a job fair. NBC Universal was hiring. We were sitting at the large conference room. There were about one hundred people.

A black employee from NBC Universal was talking about something. He was recruiting. I couldn't hear anything. Renata didn't provide any ASL interpreters. None of those jobs was for me. I didn't have any office experience. I didn't understand why Renata would bring me there. Yeah, I had the skills, such as being on the computer all day, but I still had to have job experience. Working at Kmart as a cashier and working in a warehouse didn't match what they are looking for. After the black employee finished recruiting, Renata gave him my resume before he left.

Everyone, Renata, and I sat back down at the conference room, and SAG/AFTRA staff were talking about how they needed actors. They also gave me information about how much they charge actors to join the union. The price was one thousand dollars or three thousand dollars. I forgot the exact price, but I wouldn't pay for shit like that for membership. I could see why actors are starving. Union my ass. I wasn't interested in becoming an actor anyway. That was another stupid reason for Renata to take me there. I guessed that was why actors felt they were so important because they joined SAG/AFTRA. I felt SAG/AFTRA was so unnecessary. I bet Tom Cruise was never a SAG/AFTRA member.

Then Renata decided to go home, but I wanted to see what the Black female guest speaker wanted. She asked people at the conference room to come upstairs if they were interested in writing scripts. So, I wanted to go. I followed the black woman, up the elevator, and into a smaller conference room with a long white table and a board with black markers and a great view of Beverly Hills from the window. There were about twenty people there. She mentioned something about Bill Cosby. I had to pay fees in order to join her writing workshop. She said she would give my script to Bill Cosby to read because she knew him personally. I felt like it was phony. A scam.

It seemed like most people in Los Angeles were liars. If you go to Los Angeles, please do not be naive and gullible. Do not believe what people tell you. Do not pay for anything. You're just wasting your money and you're not going anywhere. They all said, "Oh, I know this person", "Oh, this person is my family member," or "Oh, this person is my close friend." Do not go to a script festival or film festival and give your money to them. People claimed that they were working for Lionsgate, saying that Lionsgate was looking for scripts. Do not pay for anything. Use your money to make your own movies and distribute the movie yourself.

So, that day with Renata was a waste of time. I even contacted the NBC Universal staff, the black man who spoke at the job fair and was recruiting. I just wanted him to help me get a job at Universal Studios. He emailed me that I need to get on the website of NBC Universal job posting. All I saw was executive jobs with years of experience of working in the office. He wanted me to give him the resume again. I told him that Renata gave him the resume after he recruited during the job fair, but he said he couldn't find it. He lost it.

"Why bother to show up at a job fair when most people there didn't have any office experience?" I emailed him.

I forwarded the email conversation to Renata. She was so pissed at me. She emailed me that she no longer wanted to help me find a job.

Robert emailed me and asked what happened. I explained what was going on, so he decided to find some other way to help me find a job.

***

My mom had stopped talking to me, because of the stupid car and Clara and family members in California. The car, a red Ford Focus, was vandalized by Aunt Clara, Uncle Warren, an unknown enemy, or Jeff in 2011. They wanted me to go back to Memphis. I told them that I wasn't in Los Angeles because of them. I was in Los Angeles to make films.

They were so full of themselves. Clara got mad at me because I didn't visit them often. It didn't make sense. They wanted me back to Memphis, but they were pissed because I didn't contact them or go places with them. I had a life.

They lived in Carson, California, which is thirty miles away from my apartment. I had to take a city bus to get there. By bus, it would take about an hour and a half.

***

Be In A Movie, I found it on a website and decided to be an extra. The movie industry contacted them to get crowds for their movies.

Because my car was vandalized, my sister took the car away. It was my sister's car; she was the owner. I still thought my uncle and aunt should pay for the damage to the car since they said the children did it. I didn't think the children were strong enough to break the side mirror. If the children did it, they needed to contact the children's parents to pay for the damage.

I had to take the bus 603 to Dodger Stadium. The bus dropped me off on 1000 Vin Scully Avenue, and then I walked on foot in the one-thousand-foot parking lot. I was so pissed at my Uncle and Aunt. Maybe it was Jeff, ugh.

If my Uncle and Aunt vandalized my car, they knew me all my life, and they knew I had been through a lot with my appearance and all. I can't believe that they would hurt me like that. They had five children and a bunch of grandkids and great-grandkids. Why did they need me there with them all the time?

"They are such a bitch!" I mumbled to myself.

I met people at the stadium and stood in line to be an extra. I thought I was going to be late, but the people hadn't even gotten into the stadium yet. The movie industry was making a movie called *"Moneyball"*. I didn't see Brad Pitt there. I gave the leader my ticket, and he told me I could go inside the stadium, I had my blue shirt and my blue pompom shaker. About thirty people were pretending to be baseball fans.

***

Robert set me up with Cynthia at the Asian Rehabilitation Service to help me. He gave me an address which was 1701 East Washington Boulevard in Los Angeles.

It was 2012, Cynthia emailed me to set up an appointment. I rode the blue line train to the Washington Station and got off, then I walked to the white warehouse building. I had to walk around the back of the warehouse. I saw people with Down Syndrome working, they were packing and assembling things inside boxes.

I met Cynthia at the warehouse in Los Angeles. She had long black hair and was a Latina. She was average looking and seemed nice.

"Why can't I work here?" I asked her.

"Those jobs are for people with developmental disabilities and you don't have any. Plus, they make ten dollars a day," she signed.

Vocational Rehab's warehouses were working people with disabilities like slaves.

Cynthia rescheduled the appointment and asked me to come back later to search for a job online.

***

I relaxed in my apartment, watching the presidential debate online. It was very interesting. Romney and Santorum were winning the Iowa caucus. I'm a Republican and was rooting for Romney.

***

The only time I took a break from the Internet was I had to go out and run some errands or if *"The Bachelor"* or *"The Bachelorette"* was on TV. Sometimes I would watch the *"Miss America Pageant"*. *"Shark Tank"*, *"American Idol"*, *"Big Brother"*, and *"Wipeout"*, and they were getting boring to me.

***

Whitney Houston died on February 11, 2012. I watched her funeral both online and on TV. She was one of my favorite singers. I went by Beverly Hilton Hotel to look around. There I met Marlee Matlin in person at the Media Access Awards event.

I thought the hotel was overrated because the Holidays Inn looked better on the inside. The carpet looked cheap. It was just a typical hotel. If celebrities went there often, I thought it would be elegant, like the hotels in Las Vegas.

***

Robert emailed me, using his personal email address. We were emailing about sex. He mentioned Friends with Benefits. I had never heard of that.

"You're nice-looking, why not get a girlfriend?" I emailed him.

"I don't want love, my heart has been broken so many times," he emailed me.

So, I agreed to meet him at the Bubba Gump restaurant in Santa Monica.

***

Finally, Jose, the maintenance worker, brought in a new refrigerator. My old refrigerator was broken a few days ago, so the apartment had to replace the refrigerator. My old refrigerator was something like 4.6 cubic feet, and the new one was 7.7 cubic feet. It was cool because I could buy more food to keep in there.

***

On the pier near the Bubba Gump restaurant in Santa Monica, a man had about four parrots and he put one of the parrots on my shoulder. It put its mouth on my eyeglasses. He was entertaining lots of people. One of them alerted him that the parrot was messing with my eyeglasses. So, he took the parrot off of me. I smiled and dropped money into his bucket.

I went into the restaurant and kept looking at my watch. I doubted he would show up. I ordered some food and a drink. I didn't have a cell phone at the time, but then Robert came in and sat down. We chatted.

"Deaf people avoided coming here in this area," he said.

"Why? It is lovely here," I asked.

"I don't know why," he signed.

After I finished eating, we walked to his parked car. He had parked on the roof of the building on Ocean Avenue. We sat in the car and watched the ocean view. He put the key in the ignition, then put his hand on the gear shift and moved it to reverse. I reached over and put my left hand between his legs. He unzipped his pants, then he put the car in park as if he couldn't focus on driving with my hand there. Then I saw how small his white penis was. I gave him the condom.

"I'm allergic to it," he said.

He got out of the car and went around to sit on the passenger side with me on his lap. We pulled down our pants to our legs and we began to grind. He rubbed his penis against my clitoris and he was moaning and screaming so loud. I wanted him to put his penis inside my vagina. I figured I could get an abortion if I turned out to be pregnant. He nodded. We proceeded, with him rubbing his penis against my clitoris. He was groaning so loud. He cummed and made a mess on himself. He used the towel to clean up.

We pulled up our pants and he went back around and sat in the driver's seat. We laughed. Then a car pulled up beside us.

"He would have caught us," he said.

We laughed again.

"I'll give you a ride to my house one day. Where is the bus stop so I can drop you off there?" he signed.

I told him it is down there. I pointed.

"I'll show you once we are on the road," I said.

I looked back and saw two baby seats. I didn't know if he was married and had kids, but he explained that he was taking care of his friend's kids.

***

I was using the Meetup website. I wanted to meet new people because I didn't move to Los Angeles just to sit around all day at my apartment. My Social Security Income was tight because of the increased rent, groceries, and all. It was too expensive to go out. But vocational rehabilitation was sending me a check for transportation fees for me to search for a job. I felt that volunteering

would be good for me, something I could add to my
resume.

I went to a wine festival with the Meetup group,
which was raising money for charity. The event was at
Raleigh Studios Hollywood, 5300 Melrose Avenue East in
Los Angeles. I was having a good time volunteering; my
job was to collect the tickets from the attendees. During
the break, we sipped wine and ate some cheese.

The Meetup group organizer wanted us to go to
Project Angel Food company on 922 Vine Street in Los
Angeles. So, I went there, met with the group. We were
making bead bracelets; which Project Angel Food was
selling. I bought two for ten dollars and shipped them to
my mother. I don't wear jewelry.

***

I looked online and emailed the Project Angel
Food volunteer coordinator to ask when I could go there
to volunteer. I was hoping to meet the Project Angel
Food owner because she wrote books. I thought that if I
met her, I could ask if she could recommend a publishing
company to publish my book. But I never got to meet her
in person.

I did data-entry work at Project Angel Food's
office. I also helped to wrap up art for the buyers to take
home at 'Get Art' at Sunset Gower Studios. I helped to

plant vegetables on the lot at the Koreatown on the corner of San Marino and Normandie. The leader there knew sign language, which was cool. We became friends. He was a tall, white guy with a beer belly who always wore a large hat.

I met a celebrity who was on *"NCIS"*, Pauley Perrette, after helping to set up a dinner party with the Meetup group at the Project Angel Food company.

Then Project Angel Food had a "Jazzy" event at the Hollywood and Highland Center on 6801 Hollywood Boulevard in Hollywood, California at nighttime. At first, they had me serving wine and cheese. Then the next day, they wanted me to help set up chairs and tables. Then I put wristbands on the attendees. I was able to listen to the jazz music while the guests sat on the white chairs and the jazz band was on stage.

The music was so loud. I felt I really deserved to be there. After all of the bad things happening to me in the past and the way people treated me when I was young. The way Bobby and Jeff treated me, and the days and weeks in hospitals having reconstruction surgeries on my face. I really did deserve to be there, having a good time.

Since I didn't see the Project Angel Food owner and my money was so tight. I couldn't afford the bus fare.

So, I just stayed at home instead and went to the movie theatre once a month.

***

I needed to find a job, so Cynthia and I went to the computer lab and I filled out online job applications. Cynthia was clapping her hands, which I thought was rude. I don't know how many people she helped that didn't know how to use the computer. As I filled out applications, she was on her phone, texting. I didn't know who she was texting to, and I was hoping that she wasn't copying my private information.

After that day, I emailed Robert from my apartment that I didn't feel comfortable working with Cynthia.

A few days later, I was watching the space shuttle flying by my windows. The space shuttle was taking its last flight before it was retired, so it flew around Los Angeles. I thought that was the coolest thing ever. I told Robert about it in my email.

"Yeah, we were watching it from the roof of our building at work," he emailed.

***

After I received the check from Vocational Rehab to pay for my transportation while I looked for jobs. I went to William Morris Endeavor Entertainment, 9601

Wilshire Boulevard in Beverly Hills, 90210. While I was there, dropping off my script and filling out an application to become a mailroom clerk, I saw Hugh Laurie in person. The staff was detailing his gray suit.

"My mom watched you on TV," I said.

He didn't say anything. It seemed that he didn't like his job. He was like a puppet. I thought actors love what they do.

***

Robert emailed me that he had arranged for me to go to Goodwill. Goodwill was at 342 North San Fernando Road. I don't know why Vocational Rehab felt that they had wasted their money on me, but it wasn't my fault. I put in time and energy to attend this place. They blamed me for failing to find a job, but Vocational Rehab needed to find a new way to help people with disabilities find jobs.

Almost every day, I went to Goodwill by riding the Red Line train and then hopped on the Gold Line. I listened to the lecture, studied, and took the pre-employment assessment tests, passing all ten of them. I got a certificate. I made friends with the Native American man, the Jewish man, and the gay man, who were all deaf. I cracked jokes and laughed with them.

"What will you do after you finish with the test?" I asked the Jewish man.

He stared at me, then complained to the Goodwill staff member, Veronica.

"I hope this isn't a waste of my time. I feel this is unnecessary. I don't need a fucking certificate to find a job!" he signed.

Veronica was a global career development facilitator (GCDF), and she was also a personal vocational social adjustment (P.V.S.A.) instructor. Goodwill in California had a Deaf Training and Employment Center. Veronica was also deaf, a Latina with short black hair. She had a nice face.

"I will put you on the waiting list," she explained to us. "There are hundreds of names on the list. We'll contact you maybe next year or so to work at Goodwill here. We have some positions, such as kitchen staff, janitors, and computer data entry."

"I got bills to pay, I don't know what I'm going to do. My body aches. I've got a headache. I can't sleep," the gay man complained.

The Native American man didn't say anything; he was struggling with the test. The gay man couldn't seem to focus because of his anxiety and stress. I passed all the tests, so Veronica allowed me to go home early.

While I was there, I kept looking at the picture of Marlee Matlin on the wall at Goodwill. She was the famous deaf actor who won the Academy Award for best actress in 1986. She was married to a police officer and I found her home address on the white pages website. I thought all the famous actors were rich and lived in mansions. I did get to see her in person in 2012.

I hoped the deaf, white, male Goodwill staff member would help me find a job outside of Goodwill because every time I passed his office he was on the phone. He looked like someone who worked hard placing deaf people in jobs.

He was replaced by a white, deaf, young woman, though, and I felt she might not do well since she was new. I should have given her a chance.

***

At Vocational Rehab, I went to see Robert. We didn't have much eye contact, because we had sex in the car in Santa Monica. He said he wanted a copy of my social security income statement to prove that I was getting SSI. I didn't know why I should bother, because Vocational Rehab didn't help me get a job. It had been months. But I said fine. That was the last time I saw him in person.

***

I joined a scriptwriting group on Meetup. It was a long trip to Denny's near Huntington Beach. I had to take bus 460 to catch bus 29. The group met every Thursday at 7:00 p.m. I could have gone to the scriptwriting group nearby, but I liked this scriptwriting group. And I liked Denny's because the food was so cheap. I felt that I had to buy something for our scriptwriting group to use the space. It's free to have a meeting there, but I didn't want to be rude. My money was tight, but sometimes I bought something from the value menu.

One day, instead of going to the scriptwriting group. I rode the bus 29 straight to Huntington Beach. California. The place was so beautiful. I wished I could stay in California, and I wished that I was rich. Los Angeles wasn't pretty, but some parts of California were so gorgeous.

The bus dropped me off on Pacific Coast Highway near a Hyatt hotel. I didn't have a cell phone, so I went to one of the hotels and asked if I could use a computer to find out the bus schedule to go back.

At the scriptwriting group meeting, we read each other's scripts and voted on which one we should make into a film. We picked the zombie movie. I didn't help, but I was scared that I wouldn't be credited in the film. I had helped other filmmakers with their films, but they didn't credit me. I threatened one of them that if they didn't credit me in IMDB I will sue. It wasn't fair. I had done a lot of work, such as painting as a scenic painter and sweeping the movie set, helping the art department. So, I decided not to help with the zombie movie.

*****

I walked on Wilshire Boulevard with CicLAvia. They blocked off the street and allowed people to jog, ride bikes, and walk. Some people walked with children and babies in the strollers. I walked the whole way from 2619 Wilshire Boulevard all the way to Western Avenue where CicLAvia ended. Then I decided to walk alone to the Five Guys on 5550 Wilshire Boulevard in Los Angeles. My legs were aching. After I got my food from Five Guys, I took the city bus, which had to be a detour for the CicLAvia event since it had to go on Sixth Street.

*****

I volunteered to join the Women's Film Festival at the West Hollywood Library on 625 North San Vicente Boulevard. I sat in the lobby of the public meeting room, waiting for the volunteer coordinator, and watching the beautiful water fountain across the street where the Pacific Design Center was located. I was thirty minutes early.

Then a black woman walked in with several bags. Whoa, I thought, a black woman is in charge of this event. That was so awesome! I really admired her.

She assigned me to stand outside of the parking lot and direct guests where to park. I should have told her that I couldn't do that. It was hot outside, plus I was dangerously anemic. My hemoglobin level was six, while the normal hemoglobin level is twelve to fifteen. I didn't want to scare her, thinking she might not want me to do other things if I told her about my health condition. Instead, I didn't show up for that day of the film festival event. I did email her to let her know beforehand.

***

Robert wanted me to do oral sex. I had never done oral sex. He didn't give me sexual intercourse, so why do I want to put my mouth on his penis? And I still didn't know why sex was a big deal, why women had orgasms. I told him that I was busy doing other things, making a short film and all.

***

In 2013, I went to another event, for *"Alexander and the terrible, horrible, no good, very bad day"*. It was a weird title. I met Steve Carell and Jennifer Garner in person. Wow. The movie scene was filmed at Marshall Fundamental High school, 990 North Allen Avenue.

Then I was in the Rosie Perez movie, "*An American Education*", on 11710 Alondra Boulevard in Norwalk, California. I got bored with that one, sitting in the school auditorium for hours. Be In A Movie gave us a Subway box for lunch. I really enjoyed the sandwich, chips, and a can of drink.

The Be In A Movie staffer at the event announced to the crowd. "If you want to get paid, I recommend that you go to Central Casting."

I did go to Central Casting after that, but it was near 5:00 p.m., and they were closing. I didn't think they would accept me anyway, because of the way I look. Maybe in my next life.

***

A few months later, Robert emailed me that he was in Hawaii, working as a manager at a vocational rehabilitation. Unlike Jeff, Eric, Bobby, and the other guy at the Mississippi warehouse, Robert didn't give me any problems. So, I figured white guys aren't bad at all.

"We can continue to email each other," Robert emailed.

I didn't really know what to think of him moving to Hawaii. I thought maybe other deaf people warned him about me. I tried not to get paranoid. I had a bad reputation, dealing with Jeff. Some deaf people won't ever let me move on.

Nabby

West Hollywood Library Art

PROJECT ANGEL FOOD

Wilshire Royal
2619 Wilshire Boulevard
Los Angeles, CA 90057

Billing Date	10/20/2009
Unit	Bldg N/A Unit 504B
Account #	JAB-WSR200904N/A504
Move In Date	04/17/2008
Balance Forward	$0.00

Total Due	$628.24
(if paid by 11/01/2009)	

Amount Paid	Check #

19252 1 AV 0.335 ****AUTO**5-DIGIT 90057

2619 Wilshire Blvd # 504
Los Angeles, CA 90057-3454

Make payments payable to:

Wilshire Royal
2619 Wilshire Boulevard
Los Angeles, CA 90057

For proper credit, please detach and return the upper portion with your payment. Thank you.

RESIDENT ACCOUNT STATEMENT

Property Fees	Utility Fees	New Charges	Balance Forward	Total Due	Date Due
$602.96	$25.28	$628.24	$0.00	$628.24	11/01/2009

Bldg N/A Unit 504

CHARGE DETAILS *

Check

Wilshire Royal
2619 Wilshire Boulevard
Los Angeles CA 90057

Property Fees

Rent	$600.00
CEU	$2.96
Scheduled Property Fees Due	$602.96

Utility Charges:

Sewer Exp Occupant Allocation (08/15-09/15) RUBS: 1 Occupants X 6.392511161	$6.39
Trash Collection Charge (08/15-09/15) Flat Charge	$9.00
Monthly Service Charge (08/15-09/15) Flat Charge	$2.50
Water Exp Occupant Allocation (08/15-09/15) RUBS: 1 Occupants X 7.388772321	$7.39
Utility Charges Due	$25.28

MESSAGE BOARD

Water Conservation

- Use the garbage disposal less and the garbage more (even better—compost!). Saves 50 to 150 gallons a month.

TOTAL DUE if paid by 11/01/2009: $628.24

* Resident utility charges are generated by Velocity, 4200 International Pkwy Ste 1200 Carrollton, TX 75007. These charges are allocated from master property bills received by the property from the respective utility provider. This bill is not from City of Los Angeles. Charges are allocated to residents based upon their lease agreements. For detailed rate calculations, refer to your resident portal or contact the property's management staff. Property Fees reflect data in the resident ledger as of the date bills were printed and mailed. You are responsible for saying the correct amount in a timely manner. Please contact your leasing office to report any errors or omissions.

NHATE

(timeframe: 2013 - 2014)

Dear Isa,

I walked north on Normandie in Los Angeles to go and get my teeth cleaned at the dentist's office in my area. The dentist wanted to fill up my cavity, so he drilled and hit a nerve. I think that it's so unnecessary to drill into teeth. Why did God give us teeth in the first place? There's got to be another way to chew food. I paid seven hundred dollars with my debit card. Only had a few dollars left.

***

I wanted to go to the nearby food pantry to get some food, including canned goods, some meat, and a lot of vegetables. Some of the staff at the food pantry were rude to me as if only able-bodied people were permitted to get free food. Not me, who's disabled. I understand that some normal people have problems working in low-income jobs and struggle with rent in Los Angeles.

Los Angeles is overrated and I don't understand why people want to live there; the rent is too high and the houses are too expensive. I don't understand why people voted for Obama - he wasn't helping the poor at all. Free healthcare wasn't enough. Anyway, I decided to head to a hotel or movie theater to steal some toilet paper.

***

A few days later, my mouth was swollen, and I was in pain. I decided to go and see if I could get a root canal. I'd never had a root canal before, and I didn't actually know what it was. I went to the endodontist on Wilshire Boulevard but I can't really remember where - maybe nearby the Good Samaritan Hospital and Radiology place. They took checks and I didn't have any money at all. On the dental chair, the endodontist was good at explaining what he was about to do to me. He performed the root canal and then left the dental retractor mouth opener in my mouth for a long time while he went to tend to another patient. I don't remember how long I was left there, but I had to let the saliva drip down on my chin so that I wouldn't choke on it and could still breathe. I felt like Darth Vader. The endodontist came back and called the nurse in.

Scolding her. "Why did you leave her like that?"

She was supposed to stay and use the suction.

"Come on, you know better than that," he continued.

I laughed with the mouthguard still in my mouth. They turned and looked at me. They finished up.

Once I got home, I called them back and told them not to cash the check. I gave them my mother's phone number. They called her.

"You shouldn't have done it because of the way she looks," she said to them on the phone.

Which means my mother condones discrimination. My mother was black and seventy-one years old and she would holler if people discriminate against her, but not when people discriminate against me. Sometimes, she can be a narcissist. Anyway, she gave them her credit card information to pay for the root canal procedure.

***

Just because I am ugly with a facial deformity, doesn't mean that I should let my teeth fall out and not take care of my health. I understand that I need a job, but what job can I do if I have a hard time communicating with people? Let alone one that pays well and has good health insurance.

A few days later, after I'd received my Social Security Income, I went to Anaheim to get a crown. They said that they'd do it at a cheaper price. I had to figure out how to get to Anaheim using public transport. I took the 460 bus and then the Orange County bus. I looked out of the window during the ride. As I gazed at the landscape and the palm trees lining Katella Avenue, I saw how beautiful the Orange County city was. I arrived at the dental implant dentist's clinic and finally got the crown.

I sued the dentist's office for drilling into my mouth and damaging the nerve. After their lawyer did a deposition, we came to a settlement - they would refund me my money.

***

My internet was having problems. The green light on the modem was blinking excessively. I couldn't get onto the internet unless I used the apartment's Wi-Fi in the laundry room or lobby. Then the apartment building started to have issues with their Wi-Fi. I didn't understand what was going on. Maybe some people wanted to hurt me because I won't date or marry men. Or maybe it was because of all the rumors about me, about my past. Or maybe some people were just trying to bully me.

I picked up my laptop from the TV tray, grabbed my keys, and walked out of my apartment. My door swung and closed by itself. I walked down the hallway, passed the stairs, and pressed the elevator button. My clothes were tacky, and I slept in them; my mom would call me Raggedy Ann if she saw me wearing them. I hoped that nobody was in the elevator to see or smell me. I hadn't had a bath in days. The elevator opened and I hopped in. I pressed the "B" button to go down to the basement, to the laundry room. I had been doing this every day, spending hours on the internet in the laundry room, sitting on the laundry table. I didn't want to go to the lobby because of the way I dressed.

Nathan walked into the laundry room, while a Hispanic woman stood by the door. The Hispanic woman, I assumed, must be a matchmaker. She was observing. I had my laptop on top of one of the nine washing machines and I was standing up, as I was only going to be online for a few minutes. Nathan was checking me out and I looked up, wondering what was going on.

"Hi," Nathan said.

"Hi," I said back.

Then he left the room with the Hispanic matchmaker.

***

Suddenly, there was a problem with Wi-Fi again, while I was in the laundry room. I went to the manager in the leasing office, which was on the first floor.

"I can't get online," I told her.

"You have to be near the modem. Our modem is here in the office. Just sit in the lobby when using the Wi-Fi," she said.

So, I did. I sat at the ten-foot long brown table and plugged my laptop into the electrical outlet nearby. I placed my laptop on the table and sat down on one of the eight leather chairs. The mailboxes were next to the table. This was now something I'd have to do every day if I wanted to check my email, read Yahoo news, or watch YouTube.

***

I used the internet to search for someone who had written a book and may know a publishing company. While doing this, I came across Southern California Counseling Center on 5615 West Pico Boulevard. I thought that the owner of the place must be the female psychiatrist – she had written some books, but I had forgotten her name. I called the place using my TTY Sprint IP Relay service, and they set up an appointment. But that was it - they didn't tell me the name of the counselor who I would be meeting with. I just hoped that they'd hook me up with the person I wanted to see.

***

Every first of the month, I would give my check to the manager to pay my rent and take my folded shopping cart to the grocery store. Most of the time, I would walk there, but if I saw a city bus coming down the street, I would rush to the nearest bus stop and hop on with my city bus tap card. I would buy groceries for under a hundred dollars if possible, which would last me a month. I avoided Coca-Cola, potato chips, ice cream, and other expensive things. Instead, I'd usually only buy hot dogs, taco shells, beans, and pasta.

***

One day, I was online in the lobby when a tall, white, blonde-haired, plain-looking woman approached me.

"Hi," she said.

I forgot her name, but she introduced herself to me.

"Have you tried the new Nabisco cracker?" she asked me.

She pulled out the box of crackers and offered me some.

"It's good. Thank you," I responded.

After that, a beautiful blonde-haired model came up to check her mailbox.

She spoke to me too. "Hi."

Then there was Nathan, standing there at the edge of the table.

He grinned. "Hi."

He took his mail from the mailbox and went up in the elevator.

***

Whenever I wanted to go to the movie theater, I'd choose between El Capitan Theater, Regal, Pacific Theater at the Grove, Arclight, the movie theater at the Universal CityWalk, and AMC. But the one I liked the most was Cinemark Baldwin Hills, owned by Magic Johnson, as their tickets were the cheapest - maybe because it was in the predominantly Black area of Los Angeles.

I loved watching *"Gone Girl"*, *"Maleficent"*, *"Divergent"*, *"Captain America"*, *"The Hobbit"*, *"Transformers"*, *"X-MEN"*, and more. I would go and see a movie once a month because I spent most of the time in the apartment and only went out three times to pay rent, buy groceries, and do other errands. It was fun to go to the movie theater alone. I don't think any black men, especially Nathan, would watch those types of movies.

***

I saw Jeff. I saw him in Culver City, in maybe 2014, while I was heading to the movie theater on foot. I thought that he was living in Maryland, married to Maryilynn, and had kids with her.

I took the wrong bus, so I decided to walk to the theater, ArcLight cinema. I was waiting for the traffic walk sign to come on so that I could cross the street. I looked at the burger joint, where people were sitting outside at the table. They were wearing some type of orange work outfit, and I saw a familiar face with the same curly ponytailed hair. I was thinking to myself, "Oh no, he thinks I might be stalking him. There is no telling what is going inside of that Big Ego's mind." The walk sign flashed, and I walked across the street and continued walking on the sidewalk and rubbing the construction fence playfully with my right hand. I saw from the corner of my right eye; Jeff and his friends were jumping up and running like chickens. I just kept walking, pretending I didn't see anything.

***

At the Southern California Counseling Center, they'd set me up with Mrs. Trey, who wasn't a licensed psychiatrist or psychologist.

I saw the woman who was the book author. She was about sixty years old, thin and okay-looking, with brownish blonde hair. She was moving the chairs around. I wanted to talk to her, but I just sat in the lobby.

Mrs. Trey walked in from the front door and called out my name. I answered and got up to follow her all the way to the back of the building. She didn't have an office. She was just looking for a room for us to talk in. She asked me questions and I would answer, but then I would ask her a question, too. I was curious about her life, wondering if she had written any books or anything. She wasn't the person I really wanted to meet.

***

Nathan was sitting at the table when I walked by carrying my laptop. I put it on the table and asked him a question, while I sat down across from him.

"What kind of job do you do?"

"I'm a limousine driver," he answered.

"Who are you picking up?" I asked.

"I can't say who it is," he replied.

I was curious. "Is it someone famous?"

He wouldn't answer that either. I decided to ask how much they paid him.

"Enough to pay my rent," he replied.

He wasn't rich, so I hoped that he wouldn't go "Bobby" on me, I hoped that he doesn't ask me for money.

***

I was reading online about apple cider vinegar, and it said that it could delay my period. I took the elevator to my apartment on the fifth floor, opened my refrigerator, and took out a bottle of apple cider vinegar. I don't even know why I had apple cider vinegar because I rarely cook. I drank twelve ounces of the stuff from a cup and felt sick. My period never stopped. My stomach hurt every day.

***

I decided to sue AT&T and Verizon, as I felt that they had violated the ADA. I needed the Internet to call 911. All I wanted was my money back after years of paying AT&T and receiving bad service from them. It had gotten worse in 2014. The modem was just blinking non-stop.

***

I was in the lobby again, using the Internet, when I saw Nathan walking with a black woman who was wearing a dress and a coat. I don't know if she was his friend, girlfriend, or a hooker. She had her hand on his arm and he was being a gentleman. They were on their way out the front door. I continued watching a YouTube video of a food reviewer.

***

At the counseling center, Mrs. Trey wanted me to walk around the block and make some friends. I told her that I had no problem making friends, I'd just rather be alone. After that session, I always walked up South Stanley Avenue, Edgewood Place, then went up on Dunsmuir, onto West Ninth street, up Cochran Avenue, and then finally arrived at Wilshire Boulevard, where I waited for the city bus to take me straight home. You can't rely on Google map, because some streets are private. Plus, I would walk through the alley, zig-zagging through the Miracle Mile neighborhood to avoid boredom. I loved the walk and getting exercise.

I don't know why she would suggest that I walk in the Westlake/MacArthur Park area every day, it was a bad area, and being in the Miracle Mile neighborhood was much safer. I bet she wouldn't want to walk around Westlake/MacArthur Park area every day. I thought I might get robbed and kept imagining getting my head blown off by one of those thugs with their guns. A black man frowned at me while I was at the train station, buying a train ticket at the vending machine. I ran.

***

Another day, I was at the table in the lobby, loudly playing a music video on my laptop. A tall, good-looking, fair-skinned Black man came and sat at the table with his Latino friend. He told me that he was a singer and gave me his card, which has his contact numbers and a music website address. He was singing to me, but the white woman who had given me some crackers told him to be quiet. She was at the table, using a laptop on the second-floor balcony, above the leasing office. A balcony above the leasing office had an extra space for people to sit at the table. I guess he decided to tell me about his music career because he saw me watching a music video on YouTube. I never bought his music, but I did watch his music videos.

***

In the laundry room, I was washing my clothes, and Tom, a nice-looking Filipino man, started talking to me. He was usually in the lobby, but he'd never spoken to me before. He was always quiet. Now, all of a sudden, he was having a conversation with me. He was acting like we could be boyfriend and girlfriend, but he was making a lot of feminine movements. He must have thought I was stupid. He asked me to teach him some sign language. He knew some already, but he wanted to know more.

"What is the sign language for the word 'tired'?" he asked.

And I would teach him. Then he kept asking me for more words.

"Gay!" I eventually signed.

He paused because he hadn't asked me to teach him that one.

"How did you know?" he asked.

"Because of the way you move," I told him.

"Oh," he laughed.

He stopped talking to me after a while.

***

I was typing up a court paper and the complaint against AT&T and Verizon. Yeah, I was still suing them. The court process took a long time. I sued AT&T for millions of dollars. The modem's green light was still blinking every two minutes, preventing me from being online. I didn't want to be in the lobby to use the internet. I wanted to be able to use it in my apartment.

***

Another day, Nathan and I were waiting for the elevator to come down.

"Hi," I said.

"Hi," his high-pitched voice responded back.

We got in the elevator, went up, and the door opened for him on the second floor.

"I love you" a three-fingered he suddenly signed.

I stood there and didn't say anything.

***

At the counseling center, Mrs. Trey kinda compared herself to me. She's white, Jewish and didn't have a disability, so I really didn't think she knew what it was like to be different. I read about her online, and she and her husband own a textile business.

"You wouldn't hire me," I said.

"Why do you say that?" she asked.

"Because I have a disability," I said.

She was pissed but didn't say anything.

I don't understand why people want me to seek counseling. None of the psychiatrists, psychologists, or other counselors have a deformed face like mine. They don't understand what it's like to be different. They shouldn't compare themselves to me.

***

In the lobby, again, there was a young, beautiful, blonde-haired white woman with blue eyes. I could tell she was a model. She looked like a doll. She came up to a mailbox next to the table where I was sitting with my laptop.

She waved at me. "Hello."

"Hello," I said back.

I was stunned by her beauty. I wished I could look like that. I couldn't imagine how much money she made as a model. Maybe in my next life.

***

The plain-looking woman appeared with her box of crackers again. She shared them with me and I ate some. She sat down and wanted to have a conversation. I tried to talk to her.

"Where are you from?" she asked me.

"Memphis," I told her.

"Oh, you sound like Elvis, talking slow," she said.

***

A few days later, I went to the Department of Disability Office, and a deaf person who worked there, an average-looking fifty-year-old man, told me that they were having problems with AT&T, too.

"You need to go to the manager of the apartment and tell them to upgrade their internet speed," he told me.

"Do I have a case against AT&T and Verizon because they violated the ADA? What if I need to use the TTY to call 911?" I asked him.

"No," he signed.

***

In the lobby, I saw the fair-skinned singer with his Latino friend, but this time they had their laptops. They were using the Internet. I sat down next to them, placing my laptop on the table. Nathan was standing nearby. Tom, the gay man who had wanted to learn more sign language, was sitting nearby and observing us.

I wanted to ask the fair-skinned singer if I could show him the trailer for my short film. I wanted to tell him that I had made a film in 2012. I wanted to tell him that I'd like to make a music video featuring him singing one of his songs. But it seemed he didn't want to be disturbed. He was researching online about how to get rich. I felt like he was wasting time reading the Tony Robbins-like website, plus he was using up the Wi-Fi data, so I couldn't get on the Internet, as my laptop wasn't picking up any signal. With that being the case, I went up to my apartment unit with my laptop and grabbed a pen and paper and wrote, "The Department of Disability office said that you guys need to upgrade your speed so that I can use the internet service to call 911 on TTY." I went downstairs and handed the note to the manager's assistant in the leasing room.

***

In my apartment, I was lying on my bed thinking about the Internet. I was also thinking about the fair-skinned singer. I was thinking about Nathan. I was thinking about Tom. I was wondering why all of these people were around me.

The fair-skinned singer looked a little bit like Jeff, and he was married, living in a studio just like mine with a wife. And his income, he probably wasn't making any money from his music career. I did tell him that he should go on "*American Idol*" or something, but he said no. I didn't really want to deal with him again, because it didn't make sense for him to dream of becoming a singer but not want to be on TV. I can see why musicians, singers, and actors are struggling. They don't want to go up to that level or excel in their career.

Tom, the nice-looking Filipino gay man, told me that he had a deaf boyfriend. I felt like the deaf people from Gallaudet were forming a conspiracy against me.

Then there was Nathan, who stood near the leasing office. Why was I seeing him every day? I got up from my bed, picked up the fair-skinned singer's business card, and threw it in the trash. I didn't want the mess that happened to me while I was at Gallaudet, LeMoyne Owen, Florida State, or CSUN to happen to me again. It seemed like every time I was with a man, they screwed up my life. I enjoyed living in Los Angeles and I didn't want any men to mess that up by getting closer to me. I felt like people were gaining up on me.

***

At the counseling center, Mrs. Trey was still pushing me to walk around the block and make new friends, but I like being alone. I'm a loner. I feel so comfortable being an introvert.

"Love," she then mentioned.

Love is when you really want to be with that person. When you want to live with that person, or really like that person because he is funny and fun to hang out with. When I'm not forced to love him because that person is lonely, or have to love that person because I feel sorry for him.

When I was living in the apartment, I like that I didn't have to clean up the apartment every weekend. I like that I didn't have to take a bath every day. I like that I didn't have to do my hair. I felt like my life was so simple. Living in the apartment alone. Having no responsibility. Cook dinner for myself.

If I allow Nathan into my life, that would mean I will have to take a bath every day. It will mean that I will have to do my hair, put hair relaxer chemicals in, or get it braided. My hair would get so nappy... I would have to comb that stuff out every day. I didn't want to deal with that. And that would mean I would have to go out with him every day. I see Nathan as a burden. That is why I am so mad.

***

Later, I was in the lobby, using the Internet on my laptop again. I was sitting at the table with two middle-aged white women. They were chatting with me, but I could barely hear them. They asked me some questions, but I don't remember what they were asking me. I just carried on reading Yahoo! news online.

It was a nice afternoon, but my stomach was giving me problems. I was still bleeding, even after drinking another full cup of apple cider vinegar.

The fair-skinned singer entered the lobby from the elevator with a cup of coffee in his hand. He set it down on the table and asked me to watch it for him.

"I'll be back," he said.

He went back up in the elevator. I didn't want anything to do with that guy. All I wanted was to use the Internet. I got up from the table.

"Could you watch his cup of coffee? My stomach hurts. I'm going upstairs," I asked the two white women.

"Sure, no problem," one of them said.

I got in the elevator and left the lobby.

***

Next day, I went to the LAC USC emergency room, located at 2051 Marengo Street, that night and the doctor did a pap smear. I also had an ultrasound.

"Fibroid is hanging out of the uterus," said the young, white, male doctor with curly dark-blonde hair. So, I had to stay in the emergency room and wait for the gynecologist who would surgically remove my fibroid to arrive in the morning.

At morning time, I lay on the gynecological examination table with my feet in the stirrups. An Asian doctor with long black hair came in and introduced herself. She inserted the speculum inside my vagina and then snipped away with her scissors. She showed me the fibroid, it was white and shaped like a tennis ball. I couldn't believe that something like that was inside of my uterus. I was so disappointed with my body. It changed the way I felt about food. I stopped drinking Coke-Cola and eating junk food.

***

In the lobby, I did a lot of reading online about fibroids. A girl, maybe Hispanic or mixed Asian, sat at the table with me. She was waiting for the leasing office to reopen, as it was the manager's lunch break.

The manager usually left the office. The door was locked to make sure that nobody would enter the leasing office.

I didn't see the fair-skinned singer, Nathan, or Tom. I knew that they were at work. Nathan, a limousine driver, usually got off at 3:00 p.m. Tom was a nurse, and he got off around 4:00 p.m. I didn't know what kind of job the fair-skinned singer had, but he always came back at around 5:00 p.m. Noon was the best time for me to be on the Internet in the lobby. It was about 2:00 p.m. when the manager came back from lunch. She opened the leasing office door and the girl got up.

"I got locked out," she said.

The manager had to go inside the leasing office to retrieve the extra key. She locked the leasing office door again and went up in the elevator with the girl and the extra key to her apartment unit.

I looked at the time on the computer. It was nearly 3:00 p.m., so it was time for me to leave the lobby before Nathan returned.

***

A few weeks later, at the hospital, my primary doctor was doing a post-surgery checkup on me.

"I'll send you back down to the emergency room to have a transfusion," he said.

"Today?" I asked.

I wanted to know because my favorite show, *"The Bachelor"*, was coming on TV that day. I assumed the transfusion would only take a minute. I went to the emergency room and sat there in the lobby. I looked at the clock, and thirty minutes had passed, then an hour. Then it was 5:00 p.m., then at 6:00 p.m. *"The Bachelor"* started at 8:00 p.m. I thought about the city bus and the fact that riding from the ride from the hospital to my apartment took thirty minutes. The nurse put an IV in my arm. I didn't understand why I needed it. It was 7:00 p.m.

"Can you take this IV off? Can I come back tomorrow to do the blood transfusion?" I asked the nurse.

"No, the doctor will be with you in a few minutes," the overweight blonde-hair female nurse said.

"How long will the blood transfusion take?" I asked her.

"You'll be here all night," she replied.

It looked like I would just have to miss "*The Bachelor*". Finally, the nurse had me on the emergency room bed and transferred two bags of blood into my vein. I was lying on the bed with a cute white male nurse checking in on me every hour. I cracked jokes with him. I forgot what jokes they were, but the male nurse laughed.

The overweight blonde-haired female nurse came back to ask me some questions.

"Is your name Nabila?"

"No, I'm a vampire, enjoying my meal," I joked

I fell asleep on the emergency room bed and slept until morning.

"You can go home now," the male nurse said.

I got up after he took the IV out of my arm, then I went home.

***

It was around noon when I went down to the lobby. I saw Nathan having a friendly conversation with the tall, black security guard. I wanted to talk to Nathan. I wanted to clarify. So, I interrupted them and talked directly to Nathan.

"Listen, I'm not interested in you. Whatever you're planning to do, please stop it. Fuck you, man. There are millions of women out there that you could get. I don't know why you think I'm the one. I'm not going to try to figure out what kind of a guy you are... or try to get to know you because I am not interested. I don't want a man. So, go find somebody else," I yelled.

Nathan ignored me and continued to talk to the security guard. Why would he ignore me?

"You asshole! You're a fucking asshole!" I continued to shout at him.

He still ignored me and continued his conversation with the security guard. What kind of man would ignore me after I had confronted him? I walked to the table, placed down my laptop, and took a seat.

"You're an asshole. There are millions of vaginas out there that you can get. You can get any woman out there that look much better than me! I don't want a man!" I continued to rant.

Nathan continued to talk to the security guard, ignoring me. I raged on until he got in the elevator.

"Asshole!" was my final remark.

I don't understand why he wanted a woman who can't hear well and can't talk well. And my face is so messed up. There are Billions of people in this world. I don't know why he chose me. Is it that hard to find love?

I still had problems with my appearance, as well as how people treated me, discriminated against me, and set limits on whatever career I was trying to pursue. Then there were the men who wanted to make my life worse by having people hate me if they didn't get their way. Even if I settle down with a man, he wouldn't make my life any better. He would put me down instead, insisting that I was not good enough for him.

Nathan was ugly and dark-skinned black. But there were many ugly and dark-skinned black women out there whom he could get. Why not go after them? Why not force them to be with him? Overweight White women would date someone like him. He liked my personality, but I didn't like his. I was witty and yeah, I did have a sense of humor, but that was because it was the only way for me to forget the past and to make me feel better. And I ain't going to figure out what kind of a man Nathan is. Bobby, Jeff, Kunal, Pierre, Robert, and the others didn't do anything for me; they were just wasting my time. I didn't feel like dealing with another man. I came to Los Angeles to focus on films, not put up with men who treat me like crap. I didn't want some man to take away my happiness by putting me down. Every time I see men, I see pain.

I was forty-three, and I thought that I could still get pregnant after learning that a television commentator, Nancy Grace, succeeded at the age of forty-eight. I didn't want Nathan getting me pregnant and me giving birth to a child with my bad genes.

***

The next day, I went down to the lobby to browse the Internet. Rather than sitting at the table, I seated myself on the comfy brown chair in the corner, next to the backdoor entrance leading to the pool. Nathan was pretending to look for the trashcan, and he made his way toward me. He walked across the lobby with a balled-up piece of paper in his hand and then dumped it on the floor, beside me. I assumed this meant that he suggested I was trash. He then left the lobby. I thought he was going to hit me.

***

At night in the lobby, the leasing office was closed. The back doors were wide open, letting in the breeze. I sat in the chair in the corner. I didn't speak to anyone. I remember the girl who had lost her key. She was sitting on the piano stool with a Hispanic guy. A Black guy was sitting next to the back-entrance doors in the chair. Nathan was sitting at the table, doing some paperwork, I don't know how he can see in the dark because the lobby's light was dimmed. Everybody else was sitting around, doing nothing, staring at the space. That was strange. I rested my laptop on my thighs and began getting frustrated with the apartment Wi-Fi.

Nobody was saying anything. So quiet. The lobby never had over two people sitting in there. Maybe they were waiting for me to rant some more so that they could argue with me and defend Nathan against me. I ain't saying nothing to nobody. I won't repeat myself that I'm not interested in him.

I still couldn't get any signal. I got up with my laptop in my hand, walked toward the elevator, got in, and went up home.

***

The next day, the green light on the modem wasn't blinking at all. It was solid. AT&T's signal soon became strong and I no longer had a problem with the Internet on my laptop. I was happy about that. Maybe the apartment had gotten AT&T upgraded. Maybe Nathan realized that I wasn't really interested. Or maybe AT&T didn't want to lose the case. Still, it didn't make sense to pay for AT&T's service when their signal had been so weak in the past.

***

At court, their lawyer had given the judge AT&T's policy with "*AS IS*" written on it.

"They probably changed the policy," I, the *pro se*, told the judge.

I showed the receipts of me attending counseling sessions to prove my pain and suffering. AT&T won the case, but Verizon refunded my money during the arbitration.

***

When I arrived home from court, the apartment manager asked me to switch to a local Internet service which I had never heard of before. It was really strange that the Internet had started working again after I'd shouted at Nathan. I guess my intuition and gut feeling were right - I wasn't paranoid at all. It's really sad if that was the only way for him to get a woman.

***

I retrieved my mail from the mailbox and the blonde-haired, blue-eyed model greeted me with a "Hi". I looked at the manager who was clearing off the table in the lobby.

"Leave her alone," the manager said to her.

"But...," the model responded.

She was heading toward the front door. I got in the elevator. The manager continued to clear the table. I really liked the manager; she was a nice-looking Latina woman. She was very mature and looked like she was married and had kids. It was sad that after she'd told the blonde-haired, blue-eyed model to leave me alone, she was no longer the manager. I guess she unmasked the conspiracy.

***

I switched to another Internet service, Consolidated Smart Systems. AT&T was working fine, but I wanted to change it just in case. I then learned that AT&T was merging with DirecTV. I didn't watch much TV, only *"The Price is Right"*, *"The Young and the Restless"*, *"Wheel of Fortune"*, *"The Bachelor"*, *"Survivor"*, and *"American Idol"*, so I didn't need cable, and could make do with the local channels. I removed DirecTV and used a Digital Stream box that I'd bought from Radio Shack.

***

The following day, I thought that my life was getting better. No more apartment Wi-Fi to worry about, no more cute, fair-skinned Black singers to bother me, no more blonde-haired, blue-eyed models to say hi to me. No more women who fed me crackers, either. No more Nathan. And no more lobby.

I was walking out of the elevator when I saw Nathan standing in the lobby, smiling and staring at me. It was as if he wanted to accompany me. I just walked past him. I walked out of the front door, and as I crossed Rampart Boulevard, I looked back to make sure that Nathan wasn't following me. That was creepy.

***

At the counseling service, Mrs. Trey was encouraging me to walk around the block every day to make friends. She wanted me to make her a promise.

"Look at what happened to Whitney Houston. She had many friends. She was hanging out at the nightclub with her young boyfriend Ray Norwood, and she was upset because another woman was flirting with Ray! Then she died the next day from a drug overdose, or maybe she was murdered by her adopted son, Nick Gordon. I like my life the way it is. I'm not lonely at all. Why do I need friends? I can't even talk right. I can't even hear well," I told her.

I left the session and decided not to go back. There was nothing wrong with my mental state. I never saw the old lady again, whom I wanted to talk to about book publishing. Maybe I should have asked the receptionist if they could arrange for her to be my counselor. But I didn't think about it. They'd probably ask why.

***

At night, I went to the second floor and threw an egg at Nathan's door. Then again, the next night. And again, the night after that. I was so disgusted with how Nathan had tried to get with me. You can't force someone to love you.

***

Someone kept throwing cigarette butts on my air conditioner unit, which is installed in my window, from the fire escape stairs outside. It is illegal to smoke outside on the fire escape stairs. I know it wasn't from the apartment window above my apartment because they got an air conditioner unit installed on their window as well. If I didn't have the window screen, that cigarette would cause a fire.

And I kept hearing the shrieking sound of the water faucet. I saw on Youtube channel "Michael Br", how neighbors would use some type of device to annoy the heck out of the neighbors, making loud sounds to make the neighbor go crazy. I guess they use that device on me, maybe because someone hates me and wants to bully me. I thought I made myself clear to Nathan, to not form conspiracy on me because I don't like him.

My nephew emailed me. "Everyone hates you!"

Would people be happy and satisfied if I finally dated Nathan or someone that they picked out for me? If I date Nathan, I would be wearing a happy mask and taking REXULTI because I can imagine myself sitting at his friend or family member's house, eating dry chicken breast, they would be having a conversation and I wouldn't hear most of the stuff they would say. If I want to see a movie, I know he wouldn't want to watch *"Transformers"*. He would probably prefer Tyler Perry's movie. If I have to marry him and live with him, he would have to put up with me not cleaning up once a week. I really don't know what type of person Nathan is, but I know what that life will be like, and I don't want to go to that route. Because I'm a loner. I enjoy doing things by myself. I'm an introvert. I'm a dreamer. As I said, there are millions of women out there for him to be with. People can't force me to be someone I'm not. Just because I have a disability doesn't mean people have the right to control me. If millions of women are like me, then don't ostracize me. I do not care about Nathan. That is not my problem.

Nabby

FilmL.A., Inc.
1201 W. 5th Street, Suite T-800
Los Angeles, CA 90017
t: (213)977-8600 - f: (213)977-8601
www.filmla.com

Permit #F0005900

| **Invoice** | **For Estimated Fees** | Page 1 of 1 |

Bill To:

2619 WILSHIRE BLVD
APT 504
LOS ANGELES, CALIFORNIA 90057

Permit Number	F0005900	Invoice Number	00740
Production Company	P	Invoice Date	11/28/2012
Production Title	WITCH	Due Date	upon receipt
		Customer Number	200897

Fees

FILMLA FILM APPLICATION FEE	$625.00
LA CITY FIRE DEPARTMENT SPOT CHECK SURCHARGE	$85.00
LA CITY DEPT OF REC AND PARKS SPECIAL FACILITY ADMINISTRATION FEE	$150.00
Total Permit Fee	**$860.00**

Paid with Permit	Amount Paid	Check Number	Amount Due

There are no payments recorded at this time.

1ST A.D. RESPONSIBLE FOR COMPANY'S
CONFORMANCE TO ATTACHED SAFETY CHECKLIST

CK#31218

Credit Terms: Net Payable 15 days
Make Check Payable to:
FilmL.A., Inc.
Attn: Accounts Receivable
1201 W. 5th Street, Suite T-800
Los Angeles, CA 90017

Please reference your Customer Number on your check. If you have any questions about this invoice, please contact FilmL.A. Accounting at (213) 977-8600. Thank you.
Reminder: A late charge of 1.5 % will be applies to all balances over 15 days

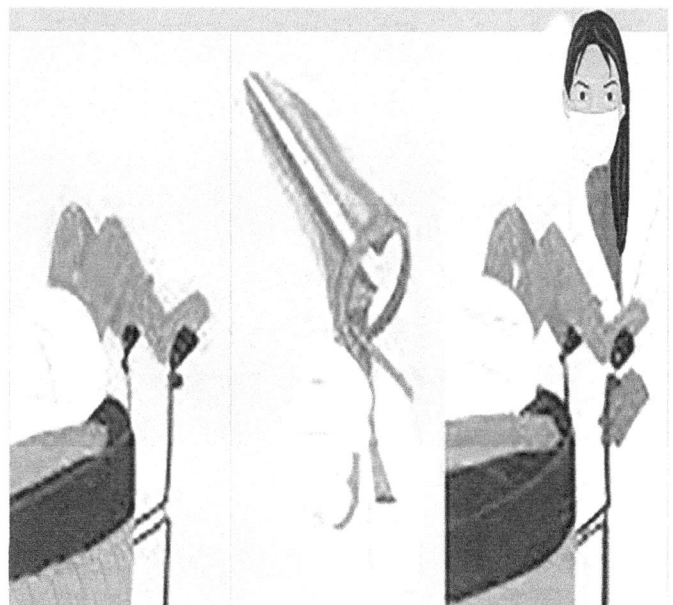

Printed: 6/12/2007 5:18:33 PM

Store 0010
Invoice # 5991
6/12/2007
Page 1

Filmtools

1400 West Burbank Blvd
Burbank, CA 91506
Phone: 818-845-8066 Fax: 818-845-8138

SO#:
Date: 6/12/2007
Cashier: Aaron
Associate: Aaron

Item #	DESCRIPTION	ATTR	SIZE	QTY	PRICE	EXT PRICE
576	Spyderco Ladybug 1-7/8"	BLK	1-7/8	1	$23.30	$23.30
678	Standard B&W Slate			1	$45.00	$45.00
4147	Cleat, 4.5" Suction Cam Mount	1/4"spud	4.5"	1	$64.95	$64.95
6228	KleenSlate 4-Pack Large	bullit	lage	1	$9.00	$9.00

				4 Unit(s)	Subtotal:	$142.25
					8.250 % Tax:	$11.74
					RECEIPT TOTAL:	**$153.99**
					Tendered:	$153.99

CrCard: $153.99 MASTER /

CUST PO#

Filmtools Return Policy: Return any item with it's original packaging within 10 days of purchase for store credit only. For items shipped by
Filmtools you must request an RA#. All damage must be reported to the freight company upon inspection prior to requesting an RA#. Light
bulbs, paint, aerosols, books, cut fabric, film, photographic paper and blank media are the exception, in which all sales are final. Refer to
www.filmtools.com for product information and return policies.

JUSTSAY

(timeframe: 2014 – 2020)

Dear Isa,

I hadn't had sex since Robert. He was the last person I had sex with, but it didn't really count because it wasn't sexual intercourse. The last time I had sexual intercourse was with Bobby in 1999. A dog has had more sex than I do during its lifetime. I had only had sexual intercourse with Jay, Jeff, and Bobby. Only four times and I was forty-three years old. I still didn't know anything about having an orgasm. I didn't want Bobby to be the last person I had sexual intercourse with, I didn't want Robert to be the last person I had sex with, and I definitely wouldn't do it with Nathan.

I went on Craigslist's personals website, where men would post to find sex. So, I thought, "what's the heck?"

"May I have sex?" I posted.

Hundreds of men emailed me. I showed some of them my pictures and deleted the emails from strange-looking men. I narrowed it down to four, and Jesse showed me his picture. He was wearing a nurse's uniform. I figured he must be healthy. Nurses have to be very healthy to work at the hospital. So, I picked Jesse.

It was the evening of October 24, 2014. I was nervous and hoping to really have good sex. It would be my first time having sex with a Hispanic man. Jesse knocked on my door and I let him in. He was about my height and he was obese, about four hundred pounds. I gave him the condom and we took off our pants. I laid on my bed and he gave me sexual intercourse.

It was cool because Jesse didn't ask me to give him money like Bobby had. Jesse didn't have me compete for other women like Jeff had. There was no conspiracy to force me to do anything, like with Nathan.

I was so glad to meet Jesse the next day, he came back and we had sex again.

"Do you want to do anus sex?" he asked me.

"Yeah, go ahead."

I had never had anal sex. He went in, and I didn't understand why gay men liked it. It didn't make me feel good. It made me feel like I had to poop. I looked down and I realized that Jesse hadn't worn the condom for the anal sex. But I didn't care, as long as I was getting sex. After he left, I was jumping up and down with joy.

"Nah, take that Nathan, I gave my pussy away to someone else and that's for having people hating and bullying me," I talked to myself.

***

On Christmas Day, there was no Christmas tree in the lobby. After Christmas season was over, in January of

2015, a Christmas decoration was dumped outside my door. It was a blue and white garland embellished with fake snow. I followed the debris of the decoration through the hallway of the fifth floor, and then into one of the elevators and down the hallway of the lobby. The surveillance camera was located up near the balcony. It could show who came in through the front door, as well as who used the elevator. I reported the incident to the new manager. Yes, a new manager. She was an overweight Latina who also had an assistant - a dark-skinned black man. I wanted her to look at the surveillance camera footage to find out who the suspect was, but she wouldn't do anything. I guess Nathan had the last laugh.

***

In 2014, while I was in the Be In A Movie group, I showed up to be in *"TED 2"*. I met David Hasselhoff at the film studio, I didn't know the name of the film studio, because the buses took us there. It was fun. I was thinking, "Haha, Jeff, this is so much better than being a housewife."

While I was standing in line with the extras, I was staring at a beautiful young white woman who was next to her stage mom. It got me thinking, "I want a child like that and also be a stage mom."

Jesse had beautiful green eyes and pale skin. I thought that we could create a beautiful child together. All I had to do was take some folic acid pills and some other stuff that would prevent me from having a child born with my bad gene.

***

Jesse and I had sex again on my twin bed. We sat and talked, and I learned that he has mild autism. Plus, he didn't want children or marriage. So, no, I would not trick him by getting pregnant. No, I would not ask him to get me pregnant.

***

I went back on Craigslist and posted for a long-term relationship, but I didn't want to be tied down to a husband and kids, though. Men emailed me and sent me pictures of their faces. Some men sent me pictures of their private parts. Most of them were Hispanic. All of them were ugly. So, I guess I won't have the baby that would look like the beautiful young white woman I saw at the "*TED 2* " production studio. I gave up.

***

I went to the doctor at my medical clinic, trying to figure out how bad my uterus was. How many fibroids did I have? What size were they? I had to go to the Radiology Clinic on Wilshire Boulevard to have an ultrasound. After Dr. Viste received the result, she told me I had many fibroids. I read that I can have fibroids removed, but Saint Ana Women's Medical Clinic was only interested in performing a hysterectomy. I think this might be because they were money-hungry, or they didn't think the taxpayers should pay for the type of treatment that only removes fibroids. Fibroids will grow back anyway.

***

I was still working on the short film I made in 2012, "W*itch*". I needed to put in more special effects. I went to the Gnomon and went inside one of the studio buildings. I picked up a bunch of postcards. I didn't really know what Gnomon was. I saw the sign that they were having an event, so I decided to go and check it out. I went into another studio building which was like a movie theater. I saw an ASL interpreter, so I decided to sit near her. There were maybe three deaf white men in attendance. I had no clue what the event would be about. They were showing movie scenes with special effects on them. I found it very entertaining. I guess Gnomon was promoting people to study special effects—animation and all. I wasn't interested in that, but the event was free, so I just took advantage and watched the movies. I also got to know some of the deaf men and the ASL interpreter.

***

I emailed Jesse because he wanted me to keep in touch with him. Sometimes we argued over how small his penis was. Sometimes we argued over me wanting to find someone disabled to love, I was kidding. Sometimes we argued over how I emailed him stupid stuff that didn't make sense.

"Coco puff," he emailed me.

"What does that mean?"

"You're cray-cray," he wrote.

"You said to keep emailing you daily, I didn't know what to email you about. I just emailed you some silly stuff I would say, Such as Big booty Jesse," I emailed.

***

My apartment building, Wilshire Royale, was being remodeled. The lobby was painted white and the furniture looked awkward and uncomfortable. They removed the table and the chairs that went with it. They replaced them with Mexican-style looking furniture. The hallways' wall and doors were painted black, white, and red. There was also new flooring that looked like a black and white chessboard in most hallways. They renovated the vacant apartment units—putting expensive new refrigerators, ovens, wooden floors, washing machines, and dryers. I guess they were waiting for me to move out, so they then could renovate my apartment unit. Then they remodeled the leasing office and moved the mailboxes to a new location.

***

Jesse emailed me and asked me to get ready for him. Sometimes he drove from his work at the hospital to come to my place. I had to take a shower, but he didn't want me to put on lotion. I lost count on how many times I had sex with Jesse, but he didn't want to be seen with me in public. The sex was good, but he liked using no condom for the anus sex and used a condom for the regular sex (vagina and penis sex). He would show me some new sex positions—doggy style. I did oral sex with him, even swallowing his sperm. When I licked his anus once, I was thinking, "Haha, now I'm not housewife material anymore." I put my finger up in his anus and rubbed his prostate. That was something I saw on porn video. I felt so experienced with sex now. Jesse gave me orgasm each time we had sex.

***

My rent was increasing every year, but Obama wouldn't increase the Cost of Living for Social Security Income. He was putting money into Obamacare. My money was getting tight, paying seven hundred dollars for rent and food, all coming from my nine hundred dollars a month SSI.

***

Jesse came back a few months later to have sex with me. I don't know why he wasn't like Nathan, Jeff, African Jeff, Jay, Robert, and Kunal. Maybe his autism has him act this way. I asked where he lived, but he wouldn't tell me. Our relationship was strictly sex.

***

The next day, after I gave my rent check to my landlord, I decided to get a government cellphone. I went to one of the booths and saw a young black man standing at the Virgin Assurant booth. I stood behind him because black men know how to shop. They are very knowledgeable about electronics and stuff like that. I filled out the paperwork and gave it to the African American female vendor.

"Do you have proof of low income?" the vendor asked.

I went back to my apartment unit to retrieve my Social Security Income document, then came back down and stood in line.

"You don't have to stand in line, I can do everyone at once," vendor lady said.

I gave her my document, Medicaid card, and Driver's License ID card. It took about forty minutes for her to activate the cellphone.

***

At night, I was cooking on the portable burner when the lights went off. That is one of the things I didn't like about the apartment. Apartment building was so old and the electrical lines were outdated.

Instead of getting Jose, the maintenance worker, I decided to fix it myself. I took a clothes hanger. I had to go out into the hallway, hoping that other tenants didn't see me, because they might report it to the manager. I used the clothes hanger to pick the door lock of the fuse box closet, which was next to my apartment door. I got inside the electrical panel, snapped the switch back and forth, then locked the door and closed it. When I went back to my apartment unit, my lights were back on.

***

A few days later, I saw a party invitation note on my door. The apartment management was throwing a party in the lobby for the tenants at 4:00 p.m. I didn't want to go because I thought that Nathan would be there. I don't know if Nathan was still living at the apartment or maybe I broke his heart and he moved away. This wasn't the first time the management threw a party. I just never went because I was too scared I'd run into Nathan.

***

2017 was a crazy year. It was wonderful to still have sex with Jesse for nearly three years. That was the longest I had ever been with a man. Jesse was the only man I had sex with many times, I think it was about twelve times. This was a great sex life for me—a long sexual relationship with him.

***

I made a music video with a white male singer who played his guitar, and I hired a pretty actress. I gave them each one hundred dollars. It took one day for filming.

***

A few days later, I decided to exercise every day to have a flat stomach, even though I was forty-six. The medical staff at the White Memorial Medical Plaza II's cancer center said I was very healthy. I was flattered by that. I don't know why my primary doctor, Dr. Viste, wanted me to go there. Fibroid tumors aren't cancer at all. Many women have fibroids. It wasn't uncommon at all.

***

Jesse told me through email that he wanted to come over at 6:00 a.m. tomorrow.

"No, I'm not waking up that early in the morning," I emailed back.

"I always wake up and my penis would be so hard," he explained.

"How are you going to come over with no car?" I asked.

"Well, I can try to ask my friend if I could borrow his car," he emailed.

"Okay, well good luck with that," I said.

His brother had taken his car away from him. He had to find a way to go to work and to find a way to come over to my place. Sometimes he came after work, during lunchtime, or at night.

***

Being In A Movie company emailed me. They were searching for black people to be in a black crowd. I joined in by confirming on their website and marked my calendar to remind myself to go. I had my calendar hung on the white bathroom door. When it was time to go, I decided to go early, I took the city bus 20 on Wilshire and it headed to Flower Street. I got off and walked down Flower Street. I saw an 'Open House' sign outside of an apartment building. One of the hostesses gave me a map of seven apartments that were having open houses. I didn't have much time, so I only did three.

I went up on the elevator and followed the arrow sign. I saw the crowd and went inside the apartment unit. It was decorated with beautiful furniture, plates, and a television. I picked up one of the cards and read the price—three thousand dollars! The window view of the city was beautiful.

I went up on the elevator to the rooftop and saw a swimming pool. A security guard was following me around, but I didn't care. I put my hand in the swimming pool, making the water wave. I grabbed one of the cans of soda that was in a small tub of ice. I opened it and drank it. It tasted like a *Monster* drink, and I didn't like it. I had enough apartment hunting. I was hoping one day to move in if I became rich. I guess it won't ever happen.

I hurried to get to the Be In A Movie event near Pico. It was a movie about Black Lives Matter. I wanted to stand behind the crowd so that they didn't have to edit out my ugly face, but the film directors wanted me to stand out in front of the crowd. I watched the crew; they were hiding our logos on our clothes with tape. I learned so much by watching the professional filmmakers and how they set up cameras and fog machines.

They had me acting a little bit, I was attacking the fake national guard with uniform and shield.

"Black Lives Matters!" I yelled.

That was a fun experiment. After that, I went home.

***

A few days later, Jesse was at my apartment again.

"Are you black?" he asked.

"Yeah, why? I said.

I guess I didn't look black to him. Hispanics should know that there is a lot of different types of brown people. Not all brown people are Hispanics. India and the Middle East have brown people. There are light-skinned Black people as well.

Jesse laid on his back with no pants on, while I was giving him oral sex.

"This cock is yours," Jesse said.

"Oh, cool," I said.

***

Later that day, I exercised and I got so hungry for no reason. I vomited. My stomach felt strange. I missed my period. I figured I must be pregnant, but I doubted. I thought that I was cursed. I was just on this Earth to be unhappy and to be people's punching bag.

I went to the UCLA hospital emergency room, they tested me and did an ultrasound. I asked for a test result paper so that I could see if exercise, avoiding meat, taking vitex, flaxseed, and other herbs had shrunk my fibroids. I saw the result, and my fibroids were about the same size. I was disappointed.

I read something bizarre. The test showed I was pregnant. I did have a dream about me holding a baby. The baby had Jesse's pale skin color.

I guess I miscarried because there were strange discharges that I had while sitting on the toilet. I was thinking, "that's must be the baby's arm or something."

So, I thought about it and wondered if I could get pregnant again. Janet Jackson, Nancy Grace, and others got pregnant over the age of 40s, why can't I?

I emailed Jesse about the test result.

"No, you're pregnant with Fibroids," he emailed. "I talked to my uncle the other day, he said you're a hood rat."

But I was being passive, I gave him a nickname instead.

"You're cute fat sugar bun," I emailed him. "You're the most beautiful man I have ever seen."

"I know I am," he emailed back.

*****

I looked up Robert's LinkedIn page and saw that
he no longer worked for Vocational Rehab since 2017. I
hope it wasn't my fault. I guess VR found out he slept
with a client. VR's rule was that the counselor wasn't
supposed to have sex with their clients. I was his client.
However, I'm not sure why he lost his job.

***

In the morning, I woke up and I was still on my
bed. I saw a swarm of roaches inside and around my
garbage can. Hundreds of them. I got up and sprayed
RAID on them. They scattered and ran underneath the
crack in the wall.

***

I decided to not pay the rent. I used the rent
money to buy sperm from the sperm bank, instead. I was
trying to get pregnant. I picked out from the sperm
bank's website for a white, green-eyed, handsome male
sperm donor. I saw a picture of the sperm donor. Maybe
I could create a child that looked like the young white
woman I met at the "*Ted 2*" movie studio. I know that I
am Black. Well, I'm light-skinned, with nappy hair. But I
thought maybe if I get a very fair-skinned White man with
straight hair, the child will look as pretty as the young
woman at the movie production.

My grandfather on my mother's side had hazel eyes, and I saw a few family members inherit that gene. I know that I have Treacher Collins Syndrome, but I could do the genetic test or see the abnormality through Ultrasound 3D. I knew it would be very expensive, but I wanted to take a chance. What? Do I have to become a lesbian or Anderson Cooper to do this?

***

I emailed Jesse what I was doing. And he didn't want me to contact him again.

"My Uncle is an evil man, if you email me again, I will have him come after you," he warned me.

But I emailed him anyway.

"You're so cute, sugar bun Jesse! You're cute when you get mad. You're big fat sexy fluffy."

If his Uncle and some of his family members are criminals, I figured the future in-laws would accept me into the family. I have a criminal record. I was the Black Sheep of my family because of the way my family treated me. I would marry Jesse, but he didn't want to get married, though. I don't really want to be tied down either.

June 2017 was the last time we had sex. The last time I saw Jesse. I only had an orgasm when I was having sex on top of him. Having sex with Jesse was getting boring, though.

***

On the door, a note from the apartment manager was taped up. It read, "pay rent or move out!" I went to get help with the eviction situation at 1301 South Main. They were called '866 Eviction'. I went there. I tried to get in at the front door, but someone on the intercom answered.

"Go around the back."

So, I went around the back, up the hill on the parking lot, knocked on the back door. The receptionist let me in, and I sat down at the table.

"I'll get the person you are supposed to see."

"Okay," I said.

I was in the small room, saw a kitchenette next to the back door. The legal aid came in and introduced himself. He gave me the paperwork for me to fill out. I told him about the roach incident. He said he will do whatever to delay my eviction.

***

I had to go get some food at the food pantry. I remembered the man who said that I could get some free food, and he and other church members will provide food on Saturday morning at MacArthur Park. I remembered them always there giving out food to the homeless people, but I never went to that food pantry. So, I went there, and the man and the other church members weren't there. I assumed the gossipers got to him. It seemed like every time I talked to nice friendly people, it seemed like toxic people don't want me to be with them.

I guess Nathan would've been like Bobby, Kunal, and Jeff. He probably would want to abuse and use me as well. I guess I attract bad people. So, anyway, I went on to Saint John church on 514 West Adams Boulevard. and got some food from there.

***

The apartment sent an exterminator at my door.

"You need to get the stuff out of the closet and move the furniture away from the wall," the exterminator ordered me.

So, I moved the table, bed, and cleaned out the closet. He came back and looked around my apartment. So much junk piled up in the middle of the studio apartment.

"Because you have so much stuff in the closet, roaches love to live in places like that," he said.

He sprayed my apartment unit while I sat on the stairs in the hallway.

Later, the apartment janitor shampooed my carpet. Then the Jose and other maintenance staff painted my wall and gave me a new air conditioner. That help from '866 Eviction' place really did work.

***

I asked my mother to bail me out and mail me a check to pay the rent. I went down to the leasing office and gave the check to the manager's assistant. He was a chocolate skinned Black man, about my height.

"We can't accept this personal check," he said.

I sat in the chair and cussed him out.

"Why not? I am not going to go to a bank to get a money order or cashier's check. That costs a fee if I get that. You guys have been getting personal checks for years. So why are you guys giving me a hard time?" I said.

"We are going to close soon. Please leave."

"I'm not leaving until you accept my check," I said.

I sat and refused to move. They called the police. The police officers came and told me that I have to leave because they want to close the leasing office. So, I left.

The next day, I went to the bank. I stood in line, waiting for the bank to open because I was there too early on Saturday. They opened around 9:00 a.m. A Hispanic woman was trying to stand in front of me.

"Don't you see me standing here? Why are you trying to skip me?" I asked her.

I was in such a bad mood. No longer passive. I sued the Wilshire Royale Apartment.

***

In my apartment, I took the pregnancy test, and it was negative. I guess I didn't do it right. Maybe I didn't thaw out the frozen sperm correctly. I wanted to see a Reproductive endocrinology doctor at the fertility clinic to see why I couldn't get pregnant. I thought about going to New York City.

***

I won the lawsuit against Wilshire Royale and received a thousand dollars check from WR for harassment. Now they accepted my personal check. There was a new manager assistant, another black young man. He was much nicer. He didn't look like an African American, maybe an islander or a guy from Jamaica.

***

I joined in Being In A Movie. It was my last time participating in them. Being In A Movie emailed me that the movie production was making a movie about Michael Jackson at the mall in Glendale Galleria at 100 West Broadway and The Americana at Brand 889 Americana Way. I went there, and I had to sit in the garage parking lot with fifty other people. The mall gave them the entire floor of the garage parking lot There were tables and chairs. We had to wait about two hours for the producer to call us in.

The producer finally ready for us, and we all walked together inside the Mall. The director told some of us to act like we were shoppers walking around, and the other half of the crowd were supposed to act like they were fans of Michael Jackson, chasing after the actor that looked like Michael Jackson. We fake shoppers had to look down from the balcony to see what was going on with the out of control fake fans.

Then we went outside of the mall at night and some of us were supposed to walk down the sidewalk as extras. A few of the other groups had to sing one of Michael Jackson's songs as fake Michael Jackson was in the middle of the crowd enjoying listening.

I was tired of standing. So, I asked a woman if I could sit next to her. I hopped on the director's chair and saw some people asking the woman if they could pose in a picture with her. I didn't understand why she was so special. Then one of the crew brought a box of a large cheese pizza to us.

"May I have a slice?" I asked.

"Yes," the woman answered.

After I finished eating, I was looking at the pretty woman who stood on the sidewalk. She looked biracial or just light-skinned black. And I wanted a child like that. She was one of the Being In A Movie's assistants.

Then I looked for the city bus 603 to go home because it was midnight. I didn't know what time it would stop running, and I didn't want to end up walking home.

I wanted to ask the woman why people kept asking her for a picture. So, I stopped being shy.

"Who are you?" I asked.

Then I looked at her, and I remembered. It was producer Suzanne de Passe who worked with Quincy Jones and Michael Jackson.

"Ohhhh."

"Ohhh, now you know," she said.

"I saw you on TV!" I said.

"I am waiting for the city bus to take me home," I continued to say.

Then the movie crew was interrupting and wanted her to look at the monitor to get her approval. I saw my bus coming.

I waved at her. "I gotta go, bye."

***

A few weeks later, I walked out of the elevator, and I saw Tom sitting on a wooden Mexico style couch in the lobby. He had his back towards me, and his head was down because he was texting on his cell phone. I quietly walked behind him. Not making any sound. I would do what a cat would do, get into position to 'surprise', and then pounce on Tom from behind.

"Yah!" I screamed.

Tom froze up as if his heart stopped. I hoped that I didn't scare him to death. He finally moved and looked back at me. He stood up from the couch.

"You scared me!"

I smiled. Then he laughed so hard.

"How are you?" Tom signed.

"I'm fine, how are you?" I signed back.

"I'm good," he answered.

"I'm going to the .99 cent store," I said.

Tom stood by the elevator as he was going back to his apartment unit. I was walking toward the front door to go out and to walk half a mile walk to the store. I heard Tom's laugh, and so I looked back and laughed too. That was the last time I saw Tom.

***

I'm not totally deaf; I wear a hearing aid. I could hear some sound. I could hear about fifty percent. People would say I hear what I want to hear. That wasn't true. I'm not faking my deafness. There are different types of deaf people. Deaf people have different ranges of hearing. Some deaf people don't hear anything. Some deaf people can hear some things. Without my hearing aids, I won't hear seventy-five percent of the sound. If I wear a hearing aid, I could hear about fifty percent. People would tell me to go get a job. I would try to get a job such as data entry or stocker so that I don't have to do a lot of communication. But it was hard to get those types of jobs. My speaking ability is poor, Marlee Matlin talked better than me. I had to repeat myself a few times because some people can't understand my speech impairment.

***

I didn't pay my rent in December 2017. I bought a ticket to New York City instead. I was saving my money for food, hotel fees, and doctor fees. Soon after I got my eviction notice, I tried to reach 866 Eviction, but they hung up on me. I guess they couldn't help me twice. They were doing a very good job helping me, I don't know why people were calling them scammers. I looked at Yelp that their business was closed permanently in 2018.

I went to the Eviction Defense Network at 1930 Wilshire Boulevard. It was near the .99 cent store. I was trying to see if I could postpone the rent like the last time. I didn't want to move out of Wilshire Royale Apartments.

I was planning on coming back after I successfully became pregnant.

The lobby was packed with people. I waited three hours in the lobby before I met the Paralegal/Case Manager, America. America looked over my application and had me to sign paperwork.

"I will email you the court appointment," America said.

I thought that I wouldn't go to court. 866 Eviction didn't bring me to the courtroom. 866 Eviction didn't give me any lawyer. All they did was get the apartment workers to repair my apartment unit and postpone the date of making rent payment I didn't want to go to the courtroom.

***

On the metro train, I got off the train at the Westlake/MacArthur Park station, and I stepped on the escalator going up. A young African American in front of me was looking down at me. He said something, but I couldn't hear him. He looked like he was around twenty-five years old. I was forty-six. He was shorter and thinner than me. We got off the escalator. He walked next to me, still talking to me.

"No, I'm not interested," I said.

He continued to talk softly. I had no idea what he was saying.

"Please leave me alone," I demanded.

I kept telling him to go away, but he wouldn't listen.

We were near the escalator which leads to the street, and he got in front of me as we got up on the escalator. I heard him saying something, but I couldn't hear him. When we got up to the top of the escalator. He was blocking me. My body was full of anger. I gave him the finger and held it up near his face. Then I noticed an obese black or mixed with a Hispanic ethnic, young woman and tapped on her shoulder.

"Do you want a boyfriend? Date that!" I yelled.

They stood and looked at me. I stomped on my feet as I was walking away.

"Leave. Me. Alone!" I yelled.

I didn't know that man. I ain't never seen that man before. While I was walking home, I had "*Don't wanna be a fool anymore,*" sung by Luther Vandross in my head.

***

In the courtroom, the judge ordered that I pay the rent on March first. I didn't have to pay the December, January, and February rent. That was a good deal. I could go to New York City. But the Hispanic manager and the Black manager assistant didn't like the deal. They wanted me to pay now or move out immediately.

***

A week later, I flew to New York City on a JetBlue airplane. I had never been on a JetBlue. I watched The Report of the Week guy on Youtube, who made a video of him riding on the plane, JetBlue. That's why I bought a ticket. Plus, it was a good price to fly from Los Angeles to New York. I loved the movie on the screen. I didn't need the headphones. The closed caption was cool. I loved the snacks and beverages. It was awesome.

***

When the plane was near the NYC airport, I got up to use the restroom. When I came back, I saw a religious TV show on my screen. I tried to change the channel, but it wouldn't change back to the movie I wanted to see. I guess religious people wanted me to watch it.

"I am already a Christian. Come on," I complained.

First, there was a conspiracy to get me to date Nathan, now someone wants to force religion down to my throat.

"I don't do drugs. I don't drink alcohol. All I did was try to live a wonderful life and try to be happy. There might not be a heaven, why can't I enjoy life now? Why do I have to wait until I die to enjoy life? Jesus this, and Jesus that. He did such wonderful things. Why can't I do wonderful things such as making movies and stuff?" I said out loud.

***

It was February. I didn't think about it. I didn't watch the weather channel on the internet. I wasn't thinking at all. February. I didn't have a coat, glove or a hat. I was still dressing like I was in Los Angeles. Short sleeve shirt, jeans, and a light jacket.

***

The airplane landed in NYC. I walked through the John F. Kennedy's airport. I took the subway train from JFK airport, and I got off of the station that was close to the Manhattan Broadway hotel.

***

Later, I looked up online using my laptop, using the hotel Wi-Fi to locate places that donate coats. I went to a church, which was two miles away, and stood in line. I was freezing, my lips were numb, and my hands were so cold. The line was moving fast now, thank God. I went inside the church, and an African American man gave me the gold looking coat.

"Do you have Gucci?" I asked.

He was confused. "Huh, no."

I was grinning.

They didn't provide any gloves. So, I bought a pair of gloves at a local store for ten dollars.

***

I went to NYC's Fertility clinics because I felt that the gossipers, Jeff and my haters were conspiring against me and felt that they want to control me. Wanted me to marry someone like Nathan or dictate how I should live my life. So, I didn't want to see fertility clinic in Los Angeles because dictators will mess me up.

I visited two Fertility clinics. I didn't like the first one, but in the second one, the doctor allowed me to get some blood tests and ultrasound. I visited the doctor three times. I had gotten my blood result, and I looked online to research about the estrogen and progesterone levels. I really didn't understand what the test results meant.

I asked the financial worker at the New Hope fertility clinic on how much does the IVF and other stuff cost.

"Ten thousand dollars to one hundred thousand dollars," she said.

I learned that the Blue Cross Blue Shield wouldn't pay for fertility treatment. It really sucks to be poor. I don't understand why people said that money doesn't buy you happiness.

I really like New York City, and I tried to get an apartment. Ugh, the apartment rent was so high.

***

While I was staying at the Manhattan Broadway hotel, I posted on Craigslist.

"Need a sperm donor."

And some men emailed me. I chose the Russian guy because he was better looking. He wasn't handsome at all, but he was white. I figure biracial children always look better anyway.

While I was staying at the hostel at International Students Residences in Brooklyn, NY, and sometimes Bowery Grand hotel in Chinatown to save money, I went sightseeing. I rode the boat to see The Statue of Liberty. I visited the 9/11 site, I went to the museum, and I rode the double-decker red bus, it took me around NYC at night. I even stood in Times Square, and I was thinking, "My future child will be on one of those flashing billboards."

While I was staying at the Bowery Grand Hotel, in a no-window, yucky, small hotel room, I was still getting emails from the Russian Guy. I told him when my ovulation began, and he could donate sperm in the cup on that date.

***

I thought about moving to NYC. I kept looking for a cheaper apartment. I did find a few, but I would have to stay with roommates. I didn't want to deal with roommates. People are so difficult to live with.

***

I asked my mom to mail me a check so that I could fly back to Los Angeles to pack up my things and to move out of the apartment because I thought that the federal court would help delay the state court order on eviction case. But it didn't work.

I flew back to Los Angeles from Newark Liberty International Airport, and it was 5:00 p.m. Public Storage was closed. So, I spent the night. My last night at Wilshire Royale. I felt sad. I was gonna miss this place.

In the morning, I paid Public Storage with my debit card, and the cashier gave me the key and the elevator code. I put my furniture, clothes, and other things in Public Storage. A bed's headboard hit my mouth as I was trying to put it on the dolly furniture mover. I didn't ask my family in Los Angeles to help me move. I felt that I was a burden to them.

I had to do one last thing, take out the trash. So, I dumped the trash in the chute, and I realized that I got locked out. The leasing office was closed, and I didn't have my cell phone. I didn't know what to do. It was 9:00 p.m. I pulled down the fire alarm, and I saw Jose, the maintenance. He ignored me, as I was telling him that I need his help. He went upstairs, I guess to look for the fire. So, I stood in the lobby with two hundred people. I went upstairs to look for Jose. I couldn't find him. The fire alarm was off. I went back to my apartment unit, and I tried to break in. I tried to knock down the door, but I couldn't. A neighbor said she would call Jose. I waited for him; he didn't show up. So, I pulled down the fire alarm again, Jose was walking up toward me. He was a seven-foot-tall Hispanic plain-looking thin man. He finally let me in my apartment unit, and I grabbed the bags. Since the leasing office was closed, I left the keys on the floor. And I walked out of my apartment unit and into the hallway.

"Goodbye, Jose," I said.

Jose and my neighbor watched me get on the elevator. As I stepped outside, two firetrucks were flashing their red lights. I walked down the street with bags in my hands as I was headed to Westlake/MacArthur metro station. Metro transportation would take me directly to the airport.

***

Once I got to the LAX, I knew I missed the plane. So, I used my cellphone to purchase a ticket from United airline website, which had a great deal, two hundred fifty dollars.

I waited in the lobby from 11:00 p.m. to 5:00 a.m. I finally got on a plane and it landed in Chicago. I sat at the Chicago airport and I felt that my brain was trying to burst through my skull. I had a headache. I took a nap on the chair. Finally, I got on the plane that was going to NYC.

While I was on the flight, I had double vision. I realized I was suffering from a head concussion because the bed headboard hit my mouth, near my nose, above my upper lip area.

I was glad that I got that done because I wouldn't get an apartment if other landlords knew about the prior eviction. The court order gave me thirty days to move out of the apartment, and the deal was I won't have my name listed on the eviction. My case would seal. I knew that I had fifteen days left, but I went ahead, packed my things up, and left to get it over with. The court rule was "An eviction expungement is a process whereby the judge seals your eviction record. Once your record is expunged, no one will be able to access it. The court may expunge your case if it finds it is in the interest of justice and that there is no need for landlords to know about your prior eviction." I didn't have to pay the three months' rent or whatever I owed. That was cool.

***

I left Bowery Grand Hotel and went back to the Manhattan Broadway Hotel and visited the New Hope fertility clinic to do an ultrasound.

"Hey, how many eggs do I have in my ovaries?" I asked the Ultrasound technician.

"Let's see," she said.

She used the transabdominal to search for my left ovary.

"Nine eggs on this side," She said.

Then search for my right ovary.

"Eight eggs."

It was so educational. I left there and went back to the hotel. I emailed the Russian guy that he can come on February 26.

***

On February 26, 2018, at the Manhattan Broadway Hotel, I placed a cup and syringe on my bed. I already inserted Pre-Seed lubricant inside my vagina. I was so ready. I had my wig on to cover my deformed ears. I had makeup on to look as normal as possible.

The Russian guy knocked on my door. I opened the door to let him in. He looked exactly like the photo he emailed me. He had brown hair with glasses, balding. He was a short, nerdy-looking guy. "Okay, I gonna have an Ariana Grande looking child. If it's a son, he'll be short like Tom Cruise," I thought. He said he worked at a computer company. He showed me a picture of his two children and his wife.

I gave him the cup and the laptop, which showed a Pornhub video. So, he could look at it while masturbating.

"Put the sperm in here. The bathroom is over there," I said.

I sat down on the chair, next to the desk and TV.

He took off his shirt, and he had hair all over his chest and back. I was thinking, "Damn, okay, hairy Ariana Grande. I really hope it will be a girl because my poor son will have that much hair on his body."

He pulled down his pants, and his penis was eight inches long. He stood there close to me as if he wants me to give him sex. I set the laptop on the desk, next to the TV.

"Okay. Just lay on the bed," I said.

I pulled down my pants. He climbed on the bed and laid on his back. I got on top of him. He inserted his penis inside, and we had sex. The orgasm was so awesome. I guess because there was no condom.

I was groaning, "Oh my God, that feels good."

He wanted me to pull down my shirt so he could see my bra. I was glad I put on the pretty bra. He shot up a handful of sperm inside of me.

"Whoa," I said.

I immediately laid down and put the pillow under my buttocks. He dressed up, picked up his stuff, and left the hotel room, and then he came back and knocked on the door. I got up to open the door. Some of the sperm was coming out.

"Raise your legs straight up, so none of the sperm will leak out," he said.

I put my legs up against the wall while lying on the bed. Luckily the bed didn't have any headboard.

It seemed like he was an expert. I didn't have to pay him anything.

The next day, he came back. This time, he was on top of me. We had sex, and it was so good. See, that's what I was waiting for, that's what I was seeking. That was what I thought actresses were moaning about. Jay didn't give me this pleasure. Jeff didn't give me this pleasure. Bobby didn't give me this pleasure. Robert didn't give me this pleasure. And Jesse didn't give me the best pleasure. A guy from Russia gave me a superb orgasm.

As he humped on me, his penis inside me in and out. I was moaning and groaning. It was so so so good. I loved it. It was so nice. I can't explain. It was like a firework. I finally accomplish my goal of having such good wonderful sex. I was forty-seven years old, and it had been so long that I had waited. I thought that was it, with Jesse. I thought sex was just nothing. But this Russia guy, wow, I wasn't expected that at all.

***

The next day, I heard a shrieking noise that sounds like the noise I heard several times before when I was living at Wilshire Royale. I had to turn off my hearing aids because it was getting on my nerves. I got up, opened the door, and looked down the hall. It was a Hispanic maid. I thought about cussing her out, but I went back to my room. I played Ariana Grande on Youtube to fade out the shrieking sound.

***

I checked my email and guess who emailed me? I have not heard from this man since June 2017. Jesse.

"Hey," Jesse emailed me.

"What?" I replied.

"What are you doing?" he asked.

"I had sex with someone in NYC, a white Russia guy yesterday."

I didn't want Jesse to be the last guy I had sex with. I would let the Russian guy be the last person who gave me great sex. I don't want to have sex anymore. I don't feel like getting naked and sucking on a penis. I am done. Done with sex. No more men. No more sex.

Jesse will be okay, and other men will be okay too. By the time the men that want me, with enemies mess with my head, mental state, and mind, sabotaging my hopes, dreams, goals, education, and career, they will be like, "oh never mind, I've found someone better." Because they thought they will never find love. If they wait, they will find someone who looks better than me. That is why they need to wait instead of acting aggressively toward me. Acting as if they will never find a wife.

And I don't want to be in any love triangle or competing for a man, because one of us will get HURT. Most likely I will lose.

***

A few days later, I moved into my mom's home in Northern Mississippi. I found out from Dr. Detti in Memphis in November 2018, several months after my trip to NYC, that Nancy Grace and Janet Jackson didn't use their own egg. I didn't know that my eggs were of low quality, or that it would be harder for me to get pregnant after learning that I had fibroids and polyps in my uterus, despite being pre-menopausal. This stuff should have been taught in High School, instead of people saying I was crazy. If I had known, I would not have gone to NYC and had visited the fertility clinic in 2018, maybe I would've dated Nathan. Perhaps I would've had sex with him and not had to worry about giving birth to a baby with my terrible genes. But after everything that Bobby, Jeff, and Eric put me through, I didn't want a man at all.

***

I read that Dr. Jane Norman, the dean of T.F.P (Television, Film and Photography) department, passed away in year 2020. She was eighty years old.

***

I'm staying at home with my mother and my parakeets, staying away from men, avoiding heartache. Relaxing and enjoying, being creative, making music, short films, and writing a book. I'm still getting email from Jesse.

To: Nabby

From: Jesse

Sent: Wednesday, September 16, 2020, 2:19:37 AM CDT

I want to make love to you.

***

Isa, you should watch the movie, "*1BR*", directed by David Marmor, that kind of like my life was, wow! Seemed like David Marmor understand.

Nabby

Garland dumped at my door.

MANHATTAN BROADWAY HOTEL

www.nymbhotel.com
273 w. 38th st (7 & 8th ave.) new york, ny 10018
212-921-9791 nymbhotel@hotmail.com

BE IN A MOVIE!

WELCOME

.com

818-985-8811

SET PASS and INFO PACK

PLEASE PRINT AND BRING JUST THIS
FIRST PAGE WITH YOU TO SET!

Pat Edwards Party of 1

Wed. February 05, 2014

Time From 9:00 AM - Till 4:00 AM

**THIS IS YOUR
YOUR CHECK-IN AND SET PASS**

ROSIE PEREZ

AN AMERICAN EDUCATION

**WEDNESDAY, FEB 5th
NORWALK, CA**

WELCOME!

PLEASE PRINT THIS FIRST PAGE WITH THE SET PASS TO BRING WITH YOU.
You can always print out another copy at

Please read everything in this Info Pack carefully. It is not that often that we get a chance to arrange
for Fans to be on a closed movie set like this.

WE WILL NEED YOU TO BE PARKED AND CHECK-IN BETWEEN 8AM & 9AM

FREE PARKING and CHECK IN WILL BE AT:

http://www.beinamovie.com/cfm.php

2/3/2014

757 WESTWOOD PLAZA
LOS ANGELES CA 90095-8358

MRN: 450744
Sex: F
Adm: 9/27/2017, D/C: 9/27/2017

myomas are mostly intramural and subserosal in location with the largest along the

left lateral aspect of the uterine

body. No adnexal masses

seen.

Signed by: NAGESH   9/27/2017 2:31 PM

Questionnaire

Order Entry

Question	Answer
1.Where do you want this procedure performed?	Radiology
2.How many pregnancies (Gravida)?	1
3.How many live births (Para)?	0
4.How many missed pregnancies (Aborta)?	0
5.Pregnancy test (HCG)?	Positive
6.Evaluate for?	
7.Last menstrual period (LMP)?	
8.Number of fetuses?	
9.Reason for exam:	VB and query OB

NYC International Student Residence

P.S. After I published this work, I know that someone will take full credit for it. I'll be like TLC, a three-member American R&B girl group, who received no money. Plus, we are living in a Jeffrey Epstein's world, when men like Nathan can do whatever they wish toward women. That is how life is for me. Unfair. I guess I'll just think like Jessie J. "*I don't need your money, money, money, I just wanna make the world* understand, *Forget about the price tag, Ain't about the uh cha-ching cha-ching*. I just want to put my life out there for the world to read." Life is a box of chocolate.... I mean, men are a box of chocolates... you never know what you're gonna get.